T0058132

THE
SCHOOL PRINCIPALS'
GUIDE TO
SUCCESSFUL DAILY PRACTICES

THE
SCHOOL PRINCIPALS'
GUIDE TO
SUCCESSFUL DAILY PRACTICES

Practical Ideas and Strategies for Beginning and Seasoned Educators

BARBARA L. BROCK • MARILYN L. GRADY

SKYHORSE PUBLISHING

Copyright © 2012 by Corwin
First Skyhorse edition 2014

All Rights Reserved. No part of this book may be reproduced in any manner without the express written consent of the publisher, except in the case of brief excerpts in critical reviews or articles. All inquiries should be addressed to Skyhorse Publishing, 307 West 36th Street, 11th Floor, New York, NY 10018.

Skyhorse Publishing books may be purchased in bulk at special discounts for sales promotion, corporate gifts, fund-raising, or educational purposes. Special editions can also be created to specifications. For details, contact the Special Sales Department, Skyhorse Publishing, 307 West 36th Street, 11th Floor, New York, NY 10018 or info@skyhorsepublishing.com.

Skyhorse® and Skyhorse Publishing® are registered trademarks of Skyhorse Publishing, Inc.®, a Delaware corporation.

www.skyhorsepublishing.com

10 9 8 7 6 5 4 3 2 1

Library of Congress Cataloging-in-Publication Data is available on file.

ISBN: 978-1-62873-770-7

Printed in China

Contents

Preface

Success is the sum of small efforts, repeated day in and day out.

—Robert Collier (1885–1950)

Successful principals lead schools in which students are learning, parents are eager to enroll their children, and teachers clamor to teach. Successful principals are able to create a community of teachers and parents united in a mission to ensure the best possible education for all of the students. These remarkable leaders have an uncanny ability to successfully respond to the changing needs of schools and students.

The pathway to successful school leadership is a labyrinth. We recognize a successful outcome when we see it, but identifying the daily practices that make it happen is another story. Although the literature abounds with lists of traits and attributes of successful principals, how those traits and attributes manifest in daily practice is seldom described.

We wrote *The School Principals' Guide to Successful Daily Practices* because there are few books that describe the strategies used by successful principals. We wanted a book filled with practical ideas that a busy principal could use as a handy reference. Information was gathered from interactions and conversations with principals in public and nonpublic schools from the United States, Australia, Africa, and Hong Kong. These were individuals who had been identified by peers and teachers as highly successful. The principals were identified by using a reputational selection process (Miles & Huberman, 1994). Since the reputational selection process is based on using the recommendations of experts or key informants in the field, we asked professors of educational administration, principals, and teachers with master's degrees in educational leadership to identify the principals they admired and believed to be highly effective leaders. The information was gathered through conversations with the nominated principals and with individuals who nominated them.

THE BOOK'S UNIQUE FEATURES

First, the book is written for busy principals who need grab-and-go solutions. It can be read quickly and in any order. Grab-and-Go Tips at the beginning of the book assist readers in finding strategies that correspond with specific problems.

Second, the book was written by former administrators who know what the work of an administrator is really like. Strategies are practical, easily implemented, and based on contemporary best practices.

Third, the inclusion of insights gleaned from conversations with principals from a variety of countries and cultures and from principals in both public and nonpublic schools offers novel approaches and fresh perspectives, and addresses the multiple contexts in which school leadership occurs.

Fourth, strategies are accompanied by questions for reflection and step-by-step action plans. These important features prompt the reader to consider pending school problems, examine alternative solutions, and establish a course of action.

Fifth, each strategy is embedded in the literature with reference made to trusted authors and researchers. Principals are provided with an overview of related literature with references that enable further research into these areas, if desired.

Combined, these features offer the reader strategies that are supported by contemporary best practices and can be adopted quickly. Additionally, the reader is encouraged to reflect on personal leadership challenges and take appropriate action.

HOW TO USE THIS BOOK

The tips in the book may be read in any order, depending on the needs of the reader. The table of contents and a section called Grab-and-Go Tips enable the reader to easily identify strategies for pertinent issues and pressing problems.

ORGANIZATION OF THE BOOK

The strategies in this book are organized into four parts—Personal, Operational, School Community, and Teaching and Learning. Each of the strategies includes

1. Tip Description

2. What the Research Says

3. What Works in Practice

4. Take Action

The book focuses on people and relationships, and is based on our belief that the role of an educational leader is primarily a human endeavor. Successful school principals have a vision for what a school can be, invest their time and passion toward achieving systematic school improvement, and facilitate change through a supportive and committed staff. The process begins with you—the leader. Thus, Part I begins with an examination of what you value and believe, the educational platform you use to guide your leadership, and your personal style and organization.

Part II addresses change—the role of the principal in initiating change, identification of impediments to change, and implementation of school change. The focus of Part III is the principal's relationships with students and school staff: hiring, development, and support of school personnel. In Part IV, we discuss the most important role of an educational administrator, improving student learning.

For each attribute, we gathered a corresponding collection of strategies used by successful principals. Each strategy has been tested by principals in the field, has been validated in the research, and is now available for you to include in your repertoire of practices.

AUDIENCE FOR THE BOOK

Designed to promote effective leadership, the book is packed with practical tips for (1) seasoned principals who seek new ideas and fresh perspectives, (2) beginning principals who seek practical ideas and strategies, and (3) university professors who prepare prospective principals.

Acknowledgments

W e are indebted to the principals in public and nonpublic schools, who shared their expertise with us, to principals who invited us to visit their schools, and to teachers for sharing their perspectives. The professional insights of all of these outstanding individuals enriched the information in this book and thereby the practices of all who read it.

We owe a debt of gratitude to our colleagues and graduate students at Creighton University and the University of Nebraska–Lincoln, who suggested names of outstanding principals. A special thank you to dear friends Jennifer and Archie for their hospitality in Australia.

Suzanne Becking, instructional design specialist and doctoral candidate at the University of Nebraska–Lincoln, provided excellent assistance in the final preparation of the book. Her efforts are greatly appreciated.

Elizabeth Grady provided first-class assistance in the preparation of the book. She "gets" writing and her happy personality and patience were a great gift—many thanks to you, Elizabeth! To J. D. Brock, who reminded us that the real reason for schools is students, we give a round of applause and our thanks.

Publisher's Acknowledgments

Skyhorse would like to thank the following individuals for taking the time to provide their editorial insight:

Kenneth Arndt, Superintendent
Community Unit School District 300
Carpentersville, IL

Betty Flad, Assistant Professor of Educational Leadership
Lewis & Clark College
Portland, OR

Theodore J. Kowalski, Professor of Educational Administration
University of Dayton
Dayton, OH

Chris Sarellas, Principal
Vaughan Secondary
Ontario, Canada

Bonnie Tryon, Principal (retired)
Latham, NY

About the Authors

Barbara L. Brock is a professor of education and director of educational leadership at Creighton University in Omaha, Nebraska. She has held a variety of positions in education, including education department chair, program director, elementary principal, and K–12 teacher. She presents nationally and internationally on topics related to career development of teachers and principals. She is coauthor with Marilyn Grady of *Principals in Transition: Tips for Surviving Succession; From First-Year to First-Rate: Principals Guiding New Teachers; Rekindling the Flame: Principals Combating Teacher Burnout; Avoiding Burnout: A Principal's Guide to Keeping the Fire Alive;* and *Launching Your First Principalship.* She has published in a number of journals, including *The Journal of the Mid-Western Research Association, Educational Considerations, Connections, Clearinghouse,* and *Catholic Education: A Journal of Inquiry and Practice.* She received her bachelor of arts degree in art education from Briar Cliff University, a master of arts with a specialty in school administration from Creighton University, and a doctorate in administration, curriculum, and instruction from the University of Nebraska–Lincoln.

Marilyn L. Grady is a professor of educational administration at the University of Nebraska–Lincoln (UNL). She is the author or coauthor of 24 books, including *Leading the Technology-Powered School* (2011); *From Difficult Teachers to Dynamic Teamwork* (2009) with Brock; *Getting It Right From the Start* (2009) with Kostelnik; *From First-Year to First-Rate: Principals Guiding New Teachers* (2007) with Brock; *194 High-Impact Letters for Busy Principals* (2006); *20 Biggest Mistakes Principals Make and How to Avoid Them* (2004); and *Launching Your First Principalship* (2004) with Brock. Her research areas include leadership, the principalship, and superintendent–board relations. She has more than 175 publications to her credit. She is the editor of the *Journal of Women in Educational Leadership.* Her editorial board service has included *Educational Administration Quarterly, International Studies in Educational Administration, International Journal of Learning, Rural Educator, Journal of At-Risk Issues, Journal of School Leadership, Advancing Women in Leadership On-Line Journal, Journal for Rural School and Community Renewal, International Journal of Learning,* and *Journal for a Just and Caring Education.* She is the recipient of the Stanley Brzezinski Research Award, the National Council of Professors of Educational Administration's Living Legend Award, the Donald R. and Mary Lee Swanson Award for Teaching Excellence, UNL's Distinguished Teaching Award, and UNL's Award for Outstanding Contributions to the Status of Women.

Grady coordinates an annual conference on women in educational leadership that attracts national attendance and is in its 25th year. She has been an administrator in K–12 schools as well as at the college and university levels. She received her bachelor's degree in history from Saint Mary's College, Notre Dame, Indiana, and her doctorate in educational administration with a specialty in leadership from The Ohio State University.

Grab-and-Go Tips

If the issue involves
Philosophy, vision, mission, image, confidence, emotions, work/life balance
Check out Part I: Personal on page 1.

If the issue involves
Difficult teachers, change, empowerment, hiring, teams, trust, appreciation
Check out Part II: Operational on page 43.

If the issue involves
Trust, relationships, context, populations
Check out Part III: School Community on page 91.

If the issue involves
Instruction, learning, professional development, teacher leaders, reflection
Check out Part IV: Teaching and Learning on page 113.

Who Are Successful Principals?

The factor that empowers the people and ultimately determines which organizations succeed or fail is the leadership of those organizations.

—Warren Bennis

Successful principals can be found leading schools all over the world. During the course of our careers, we have met successful principals in isolated rural villages and bustling urban areas. Our travels in North America, Africa, Europe, Asia, Australia, and New Zealand inform our research and writing about principals. Although the principals shared the distinction of being successful, the contexts in which they worked and their personal attributes and skills were unique. Some principals were charismatic and vivacious while others presented a more scholarly and reserved demeanor. Some led modern schools in affluent communities with ample resources, while others led schools in impoverished areas where children were homeless, hungry, and sick. Geographical and socio-economic circumstances provided different contexts for principal success.

They did, however, share the following similarities. They cared about students and were passionate about improving student learning. They sought solutions that met student needs, were undaunted by obstacles, and were unwilling to succumb to the status quo. They saw opportunities instead of barriers. They were possibility thinkers. They were confident and optimistic about their abilities and willing to take risks. They inspired teachers and developed teams of dedicated, hardworking followers and supporters.

We often read about the traits of these remarkable leaders. We hear a lot about the end results. However, little is known about their daily practices—the strategies they use along the path to success. This book examines these practices and strategies.

We begin where all leadership begins—with the person who leads.

Part I

Personal

Tip 1

Examine Your Personal Compass

Know thyself.

—Socrates

- Identify your values
- Allow your values to drive your actions
- Act ethically and with integrity

Successful leaders are propelled by their values. They know who they are, what they value, and how their values motivate their behavior. Their passion inspires others to embrace those values and follow them.

WHAT INSPIRES YOU AND INSPIRES OTHERS TO FOLLOW YOU?

Identification and clarification of personal and professional values give direction to life and leadership. You become more self-aware, make better choices, are able to prioritize your efforts, and are viewed as a credible leader as you master these skills. Individuals who cannot identify their values are indecisive and may change direction with each new idea or demanding person. Indecisiveness and lack of follow-through are indicative of weakness and a lack of leadership ability.

Values are principles or standards that support your judgment of what is valuable, important, or desirable in life. Once formed, values are the filters that guide your daily behavior. You acquire your values from a variety of sources: people who were influential in your life, parents, formal education, religious beliefs, entertainment, and life experiences. Values also reflect your generation, country of origin, ethnicity, socioeconomic status, and the geographic area where you grew up and where you currently live. Some values change during your life as you reach different developmental stages and have new experiences. Core values, however, stabilize by adulthood, although they are subject to subtle changes and modifications throughout a lifetime.

INSPIRE OTHERS

When we examine the lives of famous leaders, such as Ghandi, Martin Luther King, Jr., and Mother Teresa, we can identify the values that triggered their actions. They were admired and followed because they were passionate about their values.

Unfortunately, leaders with unscrupulous values have also inspired followers, underscoring the importance of identifying your moral compass before becoming a leader or a follower. As Coffin (1973) noted when referring to Watergate, "To do evil, you don't need to be a Bengal tiger. It is sufficient to be a tame tabby" (para. 8).

ACT ETHICALLY AND WITH INTEGRITY

Have the courage to act ethically and with integrity. As a leader, your values will be questioned and challenged. Sometimes the personal and professional values you hold may be in conflict. During times of external questioning and internal conflict, consider what is most important. As a school leader, what is best for students and student learning should inform all decisions. Family issues and your personal well-being, however, are equally important considerations.

Leaders who act ethically and with integrity align their actions with their values. They know what is right and what is wrong, and they do the right thing even when the consequences will be personally unpleasant or inconvenient.

Remaining steadfast to your values during times of conflict, criticism, and controversy can be difficult. Living in harmony with your values, however, is the path to a happier, more peaceful life. Acting in a manner incongruent with your values leads to tension, stress, and unhappiness.

Reflect on a situation when your actions did not match your values or a situation when your personal and professional values conflicted. How did you feel? What did you do to resolve the situation?

WHAT THE RESEARCH SAYS

Kouzes and Posner (2002) ask, "How can you stand up for your beliefs when you don't know what you stand for? How can others believe in you if they don't know what you believe? How can you expect others to be committed if you are not passionate" (p. 46)? They suggest, "You can only be authentic with leading others according to principles that matter to you" (p. 46).

Similarly, a study by Gurr, Drysdale, and Mulford (2006) revealed successful principals were able to identify a consistent set of values. Branson (2007) contends that authentic leadership might be possible only for leaders who have the commitment and courage to know and understand the full extent of the influential power of their inner selves. He further proposes that administrators need to engage in a structured self-reflective process to fully understand their inner selves and how their values influence their behavior.

WHAT WORKS IN PRACTICE

The principals we interviewed were adamant about the importance of value clarification and adherence. Selecting a school where the philosophy was congruent with their personal belief system was important. During discussions they often referred to their values.

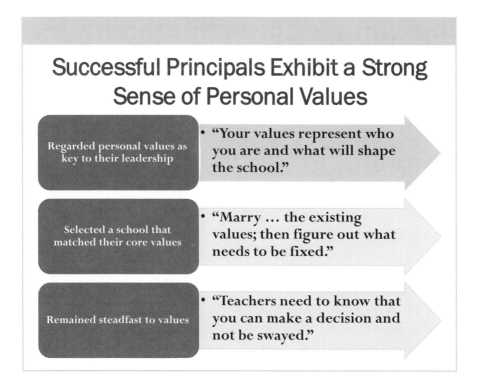

Successful Principals Exhibit a Strong Sense of Personal Values

Regarded personal values as key to their leadership	• "Your values represent who you are and what will shape the school."
Selected a school that matched their core values	• "Marry … the existing values; then figure out what needs to be fixed."
Remained steadfast to values	• "Teachers need to know that you can make a decision and not be swayed."

Following are administrators' comments:

Values are who you are and what shapes your school. It's a mirror of who we are. I never want to take too much credit for how things happen because it's certainly not just me. But the reality is, the buck stops at my desk and what happens is definitely a reflection of who I am and the vision and goals [we develop]. So it starts with me.

In one of my graduate courses we were required to clarify professional values and write an educational platform. At the time, the exercise didn't seem terribly meaningful to me. I had not experienced the role of administrator so I wasn't sure what I valued as a leader. I had a lot of lofty ideals, but few were based in reality. During the first year, however, the situations I encountered made me realize the importance of defining my values. At the end of the year I reevaluated my educational platform. I identified who I was and who I wanted to be as an administrator.

It isn't hard for me to [clarify my values] anymore. In the beginning, it may have been something that I had to grow into. When I started [as an administrator] I didn't have a clue.

I think administrators need to reexamine their values from time to time. As we encounter new experiences and grow professionally, we need to take a reality check on the alignment of our values with our actions.

Teachers want to know that you can make decisions and not be swayed.

Principals in nonpublic schools reported that they remained in their positions, often in spite of lower salaries, because of their commitment to the value of faith and school mission. One principal reported that she initially accepted a job because it was offered. Later she changed her attitude and commitment: "I discovered it is who I am. I have never wanted to go elsewhere."

One principal summarized his approach with the "Four P's of the Principalship." Principals need to be positive, patient, prudent, and prayerful.

Positive—because teachers and parents want to be around someone who makes them feel good about their school

Patient—to deal with so many people with so many different personalities and needs

Prudent—to make the best decisions for the school, not what is easiest or most popular

Prayerful—because you will meet many people you cannot help in any other way than to offer prayer for them

TAKE ACTION

What are your core values? What ideals are driving your life and your leadership? Take time to compile a list and then consider how each value is, or is not, motivating your behavior. Eliminate values that you do not truly hold, such as values that you feel compelled to list due to others' expectations. If you discover values on your list that are not congruent with your actions, identify the reasons for the incongruence, and develop a plan for change.

Use the following questions and chart as a guide. (You will find a lengthy list of values in the Appendix if you need ideas to get started.)

1. Compile a list of your *values* by completing the following statement:

   I value _____.

2. Examine the list. Eliminate values that you do not believe in but included because of societal or professional expectations.

3. Based on those values, compile a list of your beliefs about education.

   As an educational leader, I believe students _____.

   As an educational leader, I believe learning _____.

   As an educational leader, I believe teachers _____.

   As an educational leader, I believe teaching _____.

   As an educational leader, I believe supervision _____.

   As an educational leader, I believe curriculum _____.

4. In the following chart, list your values, the congruency of your actions with each value, reasons for not acting in accordance with your values, and action plans for improvement.

My values	Are my actions congruent with this value?		What or who deters me from acting in congruence with this value?	Action plans for change
	Yes	No		

5. In the following chart, list your beliefs, the congruence of your actions with each belief, reasons for not acting in accordance with your beliefs, and action plans for improvement.

My beliefs about education and leadership	Does this belief support student learning?		Are my actions congruent with this belief?		What or who deters me from acting in congruence with this belief?	Action plans for change
	Yes	No	Yes	No		

6. Write a personal values statement. Use this statement to guide your personal life.

Personal Values Statement

---

7. Write an educational platform. Use the platform to guide your actions at work. Share your educational platform with people who work with you so they understand who you are as a leader.

Educational Platform

---

8. Act on your values. Use them as your guide. They will help you stay on course when tempted to give in to emotions, social pressures, and the desire for quick answers. Demonstrating congruency between actions and professed values inspires trust and confidence in a leader.

9. Share your values and educational platform with your staff. People cannot follow your lead unless they know where you are going. Share your beliefs, expectations, and vision for the school. Inspire followers by sharing your passion and enthusiasm.

10. Stand up for what you believe. Be a model of ethical and moral leadership. Promote an environment where people are expected to do "the right thing." Be consistent in what you say and what you do. Demonstrate courage when situations and decisions are difficult.

11. Act ethically and with integrity. Take a stance and make a difference.

Questions for Reflection

- Consider the actions of a school leader you admire. What does the individual model? How are those values expressed?
- Think of a serious or controversial situation for a school leader. How would you resolve the situation? What values would influence your decisions?

Tip 2

Begin With a Vision

Strategic planning is worthless—unless there is first a strategic vision.

—John Naisbitt

- Create a vision that all can share
- Use it to guide decisions and actions

Successful principals are guided by a vision for the school that focuses on student needs and student learning. They are zealous in their efforts. Their powerful vision inspires and energizes the entire school community. Through a process of collaboration, they explore opportunities and create a shared school vision, one that is congruent with the needs of the school and focused on students.

A vision is an idea perceived vividly in the imagination. The vision for a school is an overarching, "pie in the sky" aspiration of the best that the school can become. Bringing the vision to reality requires a mission statement that provides direction for action.

The mission statement describes the purpose of the school, the target audience, and the intended benefits. It offers the possibility of action through the development of specific goals that can be measured to determine progress. A well-written mission statement can ensure that the school's vision is embedded in every facet of school life and is the driving force for all decisions.

WHAT THE RESEARCH SAYS

School progress begins with a vision of a school's potential. A mission state-ment emerges from the vision and can be embraced by the entire school community (Hallinger & Heck, 2002). To be successful, everyone in the school community must share in the vision and be committed to the school's goals. Fullan (1992) cautions against principals becoming blinded by their own vision. According to McLaughlin and Warren (1992), "The vision and mission statement must be broad enough so that all parts of the system and the community can enroll: all programs and individuals must see their place in the mission and say, 'Here is what I can do'" (p. 16).

Schools are rooted in the past yet educating for the future—a future impacted by political, societal, technological, and environmental change. Developers of vision and mission statements must be able to determine emerging trends and link the school's past traditions with a vision of future possibilities (Hallinger & Heck, 2002).

In the haste to imagine the future, Heenan (2003) cautions us not to forget the past. "The past may seem distant but it is embedded in the present and therefore in the future" (p. 1). The following story illustrates the concept:

> The old man and his grandson clambered aboard a cart to travel to a distant village.
>
> The boy, who had not made the journey before, was beside himself with excitement.
>
> "I'll sit up front beside the driver," he said. "From there I'll be able to see the way ahead and imagine what lies around the corner and guess what is over the next hill."
>
> "Not for me," said the old man, "I'll just sit at the back and dangle my legs over the edge."
>
> From there I will be able to watch the road as it stretches back towards the horizon.
>
> As we journey along, the state of the road with its rucks and ridges, ups and downs and twists and turns, will give me a pretty accurate idea of what lies directly ahead. (Heenan, 2003, p. 1)

As important as vision is, school success cannot be achieved by vision alone. The vision must be operationalized in a school mission statement. The vision statement expresses a dream of what a school can become; the mission statement provides a plan to achieve that dream. "A mission statement should breathe life into curriculum, instruction, and activities, as well as drive educational decision making" (Cook, 2001, p. 44). Successful leaders make certain that vision and mission statements are not buried in bottom desk drawers or forgotten on obscure bulletin boards.

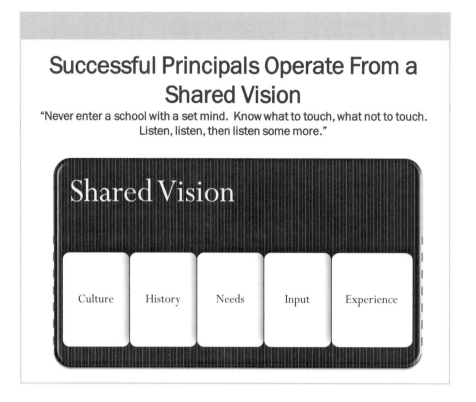

Successful Principals Operate From a Shared Vision

"Never enter a school with a set mind. Know what to touch, what not to touch. Listen, listen, then listen some more."

Shared Vision

| Culture | History | Needs | Input | Experience |

Instead, a school's vision and mission should inspire the school community to transcend self-interest and engage in actions toward a shared goal. According to Hallinger and Heck (2002), "An organizational mission exists when the personal visions of a critical mass of people cohere in a common sense of purpose within a community" (p. 12).

WHAT WORKS IN PRACTICE

The principals we spoke with were emphatic about developing a shared vision and embedding the school's mission into every aspect of the school. They emphasized how vision began with them but was developed and crystallized through reflection, listening, and dialogue with others. One principal suggested, "Be it, say it, model it, reward it."

We are the cheerleaders of the school's mission. It's our job to make sure that faculty and staff are part of that mission; that they are dedicated to it … and then spreading that to our families so they are clearly in tune and in line with the direction the school is going.

[Shared values are created by] listening and reflecting. You have the unique ability to get away from the everyday teaching, look at the tops of the trees, and see the wood of it. Everybody else is down there looking at the branches. You can step back and see [the big picture]—not just this or that class. Develop an overarching vision, share your vision and find out what you all agree on, get input from a variety of people. [You need to consider] the level of performance of the school, what people think is important, the strengths of the school, or any crying needs of the school and community. Listen, reflect, let the vision crystallize, and share what you are hearing. Get a commitment; otherwise it's your vision—not theirs. If you go steamrolling through, you will get lip service.

The interesting thing about starting a new principalship is … you can't just walk in and announce, here's my philosophy and here's what we are going to do. You have to marry yourself to the philosophy that's there and then figure out what you need to change.

When you first arrive, people want to know that you will listen to them and learn what all the issues are—what to touch and what not to touch. The worst thing you can do is begin with a set change in mind. That is unwise because it might not match with what is needed. You need to listen, listen, and then listen some more … and ask questions, encourage a lot of people to give input.

Principals emphasized the need for the vision to endure beyond them.

The vision has to be such that it endures beyond the leader. There has to be life at the school after I am gone; it's not about me. When you are absent from school, even for an extended time, everything should still function. They shouldn't miss you, although you don't really want to hear that.

Principals in nonpublic schools kept the mission alive through dialogue and modeling and making the faith identity of their schools visible.

I started with the bedrock of faith, added my own ideas, and communicated frequently with a variety of people at all levels. We make sure that our values were not just spoken, but acted out. You have to be authentic.

I keep our identity present by talking about it when I am interviewing staff, talking to parents, reminding all that this is what we are about. We are different and this is why and how we are different.

It's embedded in everything we do.

TAKE ACTION

1. Learn everything you can about the history of the school and the larger community. The vision that was perfect in your previous school might not be appropriate in your current school. One elementary principal, who failed to examine the school's past history and current needs, shared,

> I had a vision for the school—but mistakenly didn't check to see if my vision was needed in the school. I moved to a school where I was dealing with a staff with very low morale and a serious critical incident that had occurred. We had to build that staff morale and encourage teachers to take risks again. The vision I wanted was not what was needed. I needed to reflect on the issues of the school. The values and traditions in place challenged my value system. I had to deal with that.

2. Formulate a vision for the school. Articulate the vision to teachers, gather their input, and work together to create a shared vision. Consider: What perception do members of the school community have about the school? What aspirations do they have for the school? Ask questions and listen to the answers. Examine statistical data such as test scores, graduation rates, teacher attrition, and number of discipline problems. Consider the following questions:

   - What issues, problems, and challenges are present in the school?
   - What strengths does the school possess?
   - What aspirations do teachers have for the school?
   - What aspirations do parents have for the school?
   - What practices need to endure?
   - What practices need to change?

3. Write a mission statement that reflects the vision for the school. If your school already has a written mission, does it still reflect the shared vision of the community? If the mission needs to be rewritten, make

that a priority and work collaboratively with the teachers to develop one. A well-written mission statement answers three key questions:

- What do we do?
- For whom do we do it?
- What are the benefits?

4. Determine how you will measure success in achieving the mission of the school. The mission should be rooted in practicality and include measurable goals.

5. Communicate the mission statement to all stakeholders.

6. Share the mission with the school community.

7. Focus all activities and resources on achieving the mission.

8. Keep the mission a prominent guidepost for decisions. Be it, say it, model it, reward it.

Questions for Reflection

- What is the prevailing vision for your school?
- Does the vision match the lived reality of the school?
- Is the vision known, shared, and supported by the school community?
- What different visions exist among teachers and parents?
- What steps can you take to facilitate a shared vision within the school community?

Tip 3

Know Yourself;
Know How Others
Perceive You

MIRROR, MIRROR ON THE WALL

Wouldn't it be great, although a little scary, to have a mirror that revealed how other people saw you? Each of us has a self that is unknown to us, but known to others. How you think you behave may not be the way others perceive you. This unknown self can cause problems unless you discover it.

Leaders who are self-aware are better able to adapt to changing circumstances and needs. They know their strengths and they capitalize on them. They are sensitive to how others perceive them. The adage, "What you don't know can't hurt you," does not apply to school leaders. What you don't know about yourself can thwart your effectiveness as a school leader. For instance, you may think you are an outstanding communicator, unaware that teachers have a different impression of your communication skill. Adherence to your communication strategies will yield undesirable results and dissatisfied teachers. Through identification of the gap between your perception and the perceptions of teachers, you can reduce or eliminate behaviors that are ineffective.

Although self-knowledge is essential to leadership, human nature causes us to avoid unpleasant truths. Like the Wicked Witch in *Snow White and the Seven Dwarfs*, we prefer to gaze into the mirror to confirm our perfections rather than uncover the truth. According to Norman Vincent Peale, "The trouble with most of us is that we would rather be ruined by praise than saved by criticism."

Rath (2007), however, cautions against the futility of self-improvement efforts. He contends that successful people build on the talents they possess rather than struggling to become someone they are not. Rath suggests, the "key to human potential is building on who you already are" (p. 8). Focus on your strengths. According to Rath (2007), "You cannot be anything you want to be—but you can be a lot more of who you already are" (p. 9).

Begin by identifying your strengths. Ask for feedback so that you can identify others' perceptions of your performance. Feedback should be obtained from as many groups as possible. The stakeholders of your school include faculty, staff, parents, students, school board members, and taxpayers in public schools.

WHAT THE RESEARCH SAYS

The Johari Window

You may recall the Johari window developed by Luft (1970). The Johari window is a graphic approach to visualizing what we know and do not know about our own behavior. Visualize a window pane, each pane representing one of your four selves:

- Pane 1 represents the *public self*—your behaviors are known to you and others. Example: You and others know that you are an excellent communicator.
- Pane 2 represents the *blind self*—your behaviors are unknown to you, but known to others. Example: You think you are an excellent listener, but others do not share this opinion.
- Pane 3 represents the *private self*—your behavior is known to you but unknown to others. Example: Speaking in public makes you nervous, but you hide your tension so others are unaware of this.
- Pane 4 represents the *unknown self*—your behavior is unknown to you and to others. Example: These behaviors are unknown.

The *blind self* can become problematic for leaders. You increase your effectiveness as a leader by becoming aware of your *blind self*. Once you identify how others perceive your behavior you can adjust your behavior as needed.

Leaders face a dilemma when they learn information about them-selves that is incongruent with their self-perception. The contradictory information causes an uncomfortable feeling called cognitive dissonance

(Festinger, 1957). For example, you believe that you are a collaborative decision maker. Yet a survey reveals that teachers do not describe your decision making as collaborative. This contradictory information causes an uncomfortable feeling or cognitive dissonance. Aronson, Wilson, and Akert (1999) offered three solutions for resolving the dissonance:

1. Dismiss the evidence as biased or erroneous. Decide that the teachers' perceptions are biased and clouded by their resentment of the decision that was reached.

2. Change your perception of yourself to conform to the perceptions of others. Accept the teachers' perceptions and reconcile to the fact that you have not been a collaborative decision maker.

3. Use the information as a valid source of information and change your behavior to conform to your desired perception. Decide to adjust your actions to become a collaborative decision maker.

WHAT WORKS IN PRACTICE

Principals' examples:

> The only way to find out what teachers think is to ask. I prided myself on being an excellent collaborator and involving teachers in school decisions. I thought they appreciated that. However, when I read the teachers' evaluations at the end of my first year in a new school, I was shocked to learn that they did not appreciate my efforts. In fact, they thought I was indecisive. They complained that I wasted their time with discussion about every little decision. They wanted me to make more decisions on my own—to involve them only when the issues were of major concern. I guess I was overdoing the collaboration bit! I had to reconsider my approach and find a better balance for shared decision making.

You may discover some favorable news about yourself, as did the following principal:

> When I read the comments of teachers on my evaluations, I was surprised, but pleased, that many of them thanked me for my help and for just being there for them. I hadn't consciously considered the importance of those day-to-day contacts—just being there to listen and support—until I read those evaluations.

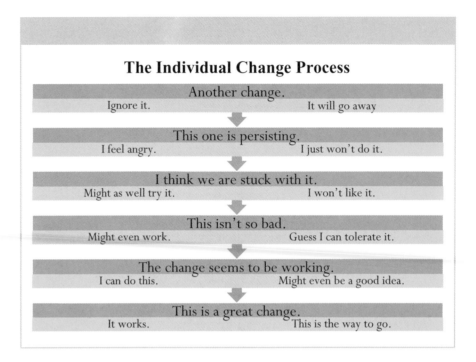

The Individual Change Process

Another change.
Ignore it.   It will go away

This one is persisting.
I feel angry.   I just won't do it.

I think we are stuck with it.
Might as well try it.   I won't like it.

This isn't so bad.
Might even work.   Guess I can tolerate it.

The change seems to be working.
I can do this.   Might even be a good idea.

This is a great change.
It works.   This is the way to go.

TAKE ACTION

- Identify your strengths using the Gallup *Strengths Finder 2.0* (Rath, 2007) or a similar instrument.
- Observe how people respond to you.
- Listen "between the lines" when individuals speak to you.
- Ask for feedback about your performance.
- Act on the feedback.

No one enjoys criticism. However, perception is reality. So, bite the bullet and ask people how you are doing. The information you receive should guide your future actions. You may discover practices that you want to retain. Ask teaching, office, cafeteria, and maintenance staff to evaluate your leadership. Invite parents and supervisors to share their observations.

Principals provided the following suggestions:

- Conduct an annual survey of teachers and staff members using an anonymous, written questionnaire. Tabulate the results and make appropriate changes.
- Observe how teachers respond to you. Reflect on the observed behaviors.
- Listen for subtle messages in conversations.

- When teachers or parents offer criticism, consider the possibility that the criticism is accurate.
- Form a teacher advisory group. Establish a regular meeting time with the group. Develop an agenda for each meeting. Invite the participation of all in attendance.
- Establish a regular time to meet with office, maintenance, and cafeteria staff. Develop a meeting agenda. Invite the participation of all in attendance.
- Meet with small groups of parents and guardians. Establish a schedule to permit maximum participation opportunities. Identify topics for the meetings. Use the sessions to showcase school successes and to elicit comments and conversation from parents and guardians.
- Form a parent advisory group. Establish a regular meeting time. Develop a meeting agenda. Invite the participation of all in attendance.
- Ask for an annual evaluation by your supervisor.
- Make changes in your behavior to improve your performance as needed.
- When you are praised for your performance, congratulate yourself and keep up the good work!.

Questions for Reflection

- Consider a time when you discovered an inconsistency with your perception and how others perceived your behavior. What was the difference in perceptions? How did that make you feel? How did you respond?
- Have you ever worked with a teacher whose behavior was problematic, but who was unaware of how his/her behavior was perceived by others? What problems were caused by the behavior? How should a school leader approach the situation?

Tip 4

Resonate Confidence

You never get a second chance to make a good first impression.

—Unknown

- Look like a leader
- Talk like a leader
- Inspire confidence
- Make others feel good about themselves

Recall the last time you met someone new. Did you make a snap judgment about the person? In the first few seconds of a meeting, a judgment may be made. Is the new person likeable, trustworthy, confident? First impressions may be long lasting. An unfavorable first impression can be difficult to erase.

As a principal, you will be on the receiving end of snap judgments. From the moment your appointment is announced, everyone will want to know who you are and what you are like. How you look, dress, stand, walk, and gesture will be scrutinized. Everything you say will be heard and analyzed. How people feel when they meet you will be remembered. First impressions can establish a foundation for success.

If you are a new principal or new to a school, you will be compared to your predecessors. People will be skeptical because you are new, but even more so if you are atypical in any way, such as age, gender, race, or size.

For instance, one female principal of a large middle school reported parents, particularly fathers, were skeptical about how well she, as a small, blonde woman, could handle teenage boys who were larger than she was. Once she demonstrated that her diminutive size had nothing to do with her ability, the skepticism disappeared. Remember to be yourself, let people know what you stand for, match your actions with your words, and give people time to get to know you.

Be prepared for visitors to your office, invitations to social functions, and required school meetings before the school year begins. New principals are often asked to "say a few words" at almost every occasion. Be prepared—have a brief, positive message ready.

People will be curious about your personal life as well as your professional background. Decide in advance how much you want to share. Maintaining personal privacy can be challenging especially if you live in a small or rural community.

Make the most of first encounters. Display behaviors that radiate a leadership image.

WHAT THE RESEARCH SAYS

Lasting impressions are made during the first seconds of a meeting. Impressions may be made in the first four seconds according to Siegel (1998) or in the first seven to seventeen seconds according to Lampton (2002).

Since you can say little during those first few seconds, early judgments are based heavily on appearance (Minnesota Department of Employment and Economic Services, 2008). Five factors contribute to first impressions: clothes, gestures, movement, stance, and eye contact. Of these factors, clothes, stance, and eye contact are the most important (Siegel, 1998).

To project a professional image, invest in professional clothing that makes you feel confident; have your clothes properly tailored; pay attention to the condition of your shoes; and dress conservatively and appropriately for the place and the occasion (Siegel, 1998). Your appearance conveys your perception of the importance of the occasion and your level of respect for the people in attendance.

Stance contributes to credibility. When addressing a group, stand up straight with your feet at shoulder width and pointed straight ahead. Stand in front of the audience instead of behind a podium. Begin your presentation by standing silently for a few moments, take a deep breath to center yourself, find a friendly face, and begin. Pick one person and share a complete thought; then move on to another person and repeat the process (Siegel, 1998). Looking over the heads of the audience or using a shotgun approach of darting glances at the audience conveys nervousness.

When you meet people, make them the center of attention. Heed the words of Henry Ford, who reminds us, "A bore is a fellow who opens his mouth and puts his *feats* in it." Instead of waiting for people to come to you, take the initiative and approach them. Be the first to smile, extend your hand, and identify yourself (Siegel, 1998).

Research suggests that a firm handshake is an effective form of self-promotion—especially for women (Chaplin, Phillips, Brown, Clanton, & Stein, 2000). Demonstrate that the person you are meeting is the center of attention and conversation. Listen to the other person; avoid talking about yourself. Use questions and prompts to keep the conversation going. Maintain steady eye contact. Be careful not to look over their shoulder to see who else is waiting to talk with you. Personalize the conversation by repeating the person's name throughout the conversation (Lampton, 2002).

Keep the conversation light and friendly. If the person you are meeting brings up a problem or concern, suggest meeting privately at a later time to discuss it. Be sure to follow through. Avoid verbal disagreements with anyone you have just met until you have established credibility. Be cautious when using humor and jokes until you know people well. Stories that are amusing to some people may be offensive to others (Lampton, 2002).

If you are asked to speak to a group, remember listeners judge your intelligence and leadership by the words you choose and how you say them. Lampton (2002) suggests you speak to be heard, enunciate, alter your pitch, and display animation in voice and gesture.

Keep in mind that your office is a reflection of you. Consider the image it projects to visitors. A clean, organized, and attractive office conveys a positive image. If your visitors encounter a desk overflowing with papers, stacks of files on the floor, and dead plants on the window ledge, they might question your ability to lead.

WHAT WORKS IN PRACTICE

Successful principals we observed project an impression that they are trust-worthy, capable, and interested in others. They look, act, and talk like leaders. They are professionally groomed and dressed, and appear confident, poised, and calm. They are articulate in sharing their ideas, and passionate when they talk about the school and students. They listen respectfully to their col-leagues, acknowledge alternative points of view, and are politely assertive when disagreeing and stating their viewpoints. Among principals who knew each other, there was good humor and teasing. When they recounted mistakes they made, they were able to laugh at themselves. The offices of principals we visited were clean, organized, and attractive, and projected a sense of professionalism.

TAKE ACTION

Every time you smile at someone, it is an action of love, a gift to that person, a beautiful thing.

—Mother Teresa

Strive to create a personal presence that inspires others. Ask yourself, do I look and act like the kind of person I would trust as a leader?

1. Do I look professional?

   - Dress conservatively and appropriately.
   - Be sure your grooming is impeccable.
   - Exude a confident and relaxed manner—even if you do not feel that way.

2. Do I display interest in others?

   - Smile.
   - Work the crowd.
   - Speak to everyone.
   - Listen.
   - Make people feel comfortable.
   - Arrange appointments for individuals who want to share problems.
   - Make no promises on the spot—not even *seemingly* minor ones.

3. Do I speak skillfully?

   - Speak to be heard by all.
   - Alter your pitch to avoid a monotone voice.
   - Enunciate your words.
   - Display animation in your tone and gestures.
   - Know when to be silent.

4. Do I speak confidently and enthusiastically?

   - Be prepared to *say a few words* if asked.
   - Make positive remarks about the school, community, and people.
   - Express enthusiasm about the future of the school.
   - Express confidence in your ability to lead the school.
   - Do not make comparisons to your previous school.
   - Say nothing negative about the previous principal.

Questions for Reflection

- Consider a person in a leadership position who made a favorable first impression. What were the factors and attributes that made you think favorably about the person?
- Think of an individual who made an unfavorable first impression, but who you later came to admire. What could that individual have done differently to evoke a more favorable first impression?

Tip 5

Master Your Emotions

Chicken Little was in the woods one day when an acorn fell on her head. "Oh my goodness," Chicken Little said, "the sky is falling. I must go and tell the king!"

—Folk tale

The phrase "the sky is falling" is linked to the errant alarmist who creates needless hysteria. Like Chicken Little, some school leaders have difficulty keeping emotions in check. Their unpredictable behavior and frequent upsets and outbursts create tension, concern, and unrest in schools.

Successful leaders possess a sense of self-awareness, mastery of their emotions, and knowledge of how their actions and emotions impact others. They know that intentionally or unintentionally, a leader's emotional overtones broadcast throughout the school in ever-widening ripples. They are the calm at the center of the storm, the reassuring presence after a disaster, and the tireless cheerleader for the weary. Teachers trust them to deliver factual information without the filters of personal emotion.

Successful leaders also know that there are times when expressing personal emotion is important. Laughing, having fun, and celebrating accomplishments, as well as mourning together during times of loss and sorrow, are important to building relationships and community.

WHAT THE RESEARCH SAYS

In calm waters every ship has a good captain.

—Swedish proverb

School leaders seldom experience calm waters. Instead, they must be able to thrive in conditions that Vail (1996) described as "permanent white water." Recent studies suggest that successful navigation of the white waters of school leadership requires a brilliant IQ combined with an equally brilliant EQ.

Emotional intelligence (EQ) is a multidimensional construct that has been likened to one's intelligence quotient (IQ); the abilities, however, are different and distinct. The concept of emotional intelligence was first presented by Salovey and Mayer in 1990 and popularized by Goleman in 1995.

Salovey and Mayer (1990) defined emotional intelligence as the ability to perceive emotions, to use emotion to facilitate thought, to understand emotions, and to regulate emotions to promote emotional and intellectual growth. Leaders with high emotional intelligence turn emotional data into useful information for decision making and action. In other words, they regulate and use their emotions rather than being controlled and victimized by them.

Everyone possesses emotional intelligence to some degree. However, this is an ability that can be developed. You can increase your emotional intelligence by being more aware of your feelings, processing emotional information, becoming more discerning about your choices, and deliberately blending facts with feelings to make better choices. Valuing emotions as a source of information will yield more positive relationships and better decisions.

According to Riggio and Reichard (2008), a combination of emotional intelligence and social skills, commonly called people skills, are critical for successful leadership. They suggest these skills can be improved through training and offer the following framework of skills and corresponding effective behaviors.

- Emotional expressiveness—motivating others and conveying positive regard
- Emotional sensitivity—understanding needs and feelings of others; ability to establish rapport
- Emotional control—regulating and masking expression of strong emotions
- Social expressiveness—active listening and monitoring social behavior
- Social control—managing leader impression, tact, self-efficacy

Leaders need to monitor their feelings and thoughts, their interpretations of others, their response to actions taken by others, their motives for behavior, and their inclination toward the use of defense mechanisms, such as denial, repression, and avoidance (Albano, 2008).

WHAT WORKS IN PRACTICE

Principals offered the following advice:

Leave your personal problems in the parking lot and tune in to the nuances of what is occurring in the school. Every person in the school is already carrying a backpack of personal issues. Do not add to their burden. Put a smile on your face and in your voice, and make school the happiest place in their day.

If the principal flies off the handle and is impatient, that behavior could develop into the culture of the school. Things won't always go as planned as schools are filled with people; you have to be patient and roll with it.

Be attuned to the climate of the building, the perceptions of people, their reactions to you, and the subtle hints of change.

Laugh with students and staff.

When you need to express outrage, disappointment, or correct a behavior, do so in private and without losing control of your emotions. If you feel you cannot remain in control, postpone the conversation until later. Angry outbursts and biting criticism magnify rather than resolve problems.

Do not take everything personally. You need to put a glass wall in front of you when you listen to what people are saying. They are going to say it anyway; if you interrupt, they will say it [behind your back]. So let it all come out; but listen in an objective fashion. This is a learned skill, but also a survival skill. I once had a parent tell me, "The school's gone downhill since you got here!" It was tough to hear. But I was able to dismiss the feelings because I had confidence in what I was doing.

The principal cannot take things personally. You won't win everyone over, but [you can take solace from knowing that] you are doing what is best for the school and students.

TAKE ACTION

"Keep calm and carry on." This popular poster, found all over Britain during World War II, contains sage advice for principals who are besieged daily with a multitude of problems. Leaders who are aware of the feelings that underscore and inform their behavior are more likely to regulate and use them to their advantage. Be like the duck, gliding smoothly along while paddling madly beneath the surface. Take stock of how you use emotions.

1. Think of a leader you admire. What emotional behaviors does the person display? How does this emotional behavior support his or her effectiveness as a leader? How can you emulate this behavior?

2. Which of the following emotional behaviors do you need to improve?

   - Motivating or inspiring others
   - Gaining rapport by increased sensitivity to feelings and needs
   - Regulating, masking, or stifling expression of strong emotion
   - Becoming an active listener
   - Regulating social behavior
   - Presenting the demeanor of a confident leader

3. What actions can you take to improve each of the behaviors you selected?

Questions for Reflection

- Which of these adjectives would your staff use to describe your emotional level?
  - Grumpy or happy
  - Negative or positive
  - Emotionally unpredictable or emotionally predictable
  - Insensitive or sensitive to feelings of others
  - Unaware or aware of group feelings
  - Complaining or uncomplaining
  - Critical or encouraging
  - Nervous or calm
  - Out of control or in control

- When was the last time you examined your emotions and the impact they had on a decision or action?
- What clues do you use to know how people feel when they speak to you?
- How did you behave during the last school crisis or major problem? How would the staff describe your behavior?
- How did you behave the last time a staff member made a serious error?
- How did you respond the last time a staff member came to you with a serious personal problem?
- When was the last time you laughed or shared a funny story with a staff member?
- How did you behave the last time you were angry or disappointed?
- How did you behave the last time you were worried or under stress?
- What is your favorite defense mechanism? How do you know when you are using it?

Tip 6

Maintain a Work–Life Perspective That Sustains Your Well-Being

Happiness cannot be traveled to, owned, earned, worn or consumed. Happiness is the spiritual experience of living every minute with love, grace and gratitude.

—Denis Waitley

The work of a principal can consume every waking moment. Principals can become so preoccupied with their work that it overshadows every other facet of their life. Some principals become martyrs to the profession, boasting about their long days and working weekends. Other principals are silent sufferers who cannot mentally leave their work; their personal lives are consumed by work-related thoughts and worries. Either way, the stress they generate for themselves and for those around them is harmful to their health and relationships.

Successful principals are able to put their work into perspective. Reminded of the moral in Aesop's fable of the golden goose, they realize that they are the golden goose, the source of their own success. They know that their ability to give to others requires sustained personal physical, mental, and spiritual well-being. Although they are passionate about their job, they do not allow work to consume their lives. They are emotionally honest with themselves, know what they need to maintain equilibrium, and take action on their own behalf. They set aside time to care for their physical, mental, and spiritual health. They spend time with family and friends. When they are home, problems at work are set aside.

The principals we talked with said that the ability to balance their professional and personal lives was an important factor in their success. By contrast, principals who *live their job* run the risk of job burnout, health problems, loss of personal relationships, and possibly shortened careers. One of the principals explained, "You cannot … take care of people in the school if you don't take care of yourself and the people at home."

WHAT THE RESEARCH SAYS

If you ask people what they want out of life, most will answer happiness or a satisfying life. "The pursuit of happiness" is a commonly held goal. The notion of life satisfaction stems from the Aristotelian ethical model of eudemonism (derived from *eudemonia*, the Greek word for "happiness") that maintains that virtue or correct actions lead to well-being and the ultimate goal of happiness ("Eudaimonism," n.d.).

Work is a central life interest and plays a major role in our level of life satisfaction (Dubin, 1956). School leaders devote enormous amounts of time, energy, and education to their jobs to the extent that, for some, their work is their identity. Family, and more important, the balance between work life and family life is equally valuable. Research indicates that the higher the level of conflict that exists between one's work life and family life, the lower the level of life satisfaction (Allen, Herst, Bruck, & Sutton, 2000; Kossek & Ozeki, 1998).

Finding a proper balance in personal and professional life is important to well-being. However, finding that balance between work and family life has become increasingly elusive for school leaders. The school leader's work has grown increasingly complex and demanding in terms of job requirements, context, accountability, and time (Gronn & Rawlings-Sanaei, 2003). School leaders spend long hours at work under stressful conditions, often to the detriment of family and social relationships.

Although potentially satisfying, the work of a school leader is also highly stressful. Leadership by definition is an emotional undertaking (Beatty, 2006). Leaders make changes that disturb the status quo thereby threatening the security and comfort zones for themselves and others. A natural outcome of change is strong emotions that can lead to conflict and stress for school leaders.

Many school leaders experience emotions such as loneliness, isolation, disempowerment, lack of control, and lack of affirmation. Rather than sharing the emotions, they keep the feelings concealed behind a mask of serenity (O'Connor, 2004). Although the emotional toll experienced is great, the normative rule of silence requires them to mask emotions and stoically deal with their discomfort and the emotional distress of others (Beatty, 2006). They adopt a demeanor of being in control (O'Connor, 2004) that stifles their emotions. Instead of disappearing, stifled emotions erode the spirit and undermine self-confidence, eventually causing stress that damages mind, body, relationships, and careers.

To sustain their well-being, leaders need to abandon the silent suffering and find outlets for sharing emotions. Emotions are an important source of knowledge about self and others. Exploring and sharing emotions are essential to a leader's well-being and success (Beatty, 2006).

Leaders who reconnect with themselves, their families, and their peers will decrease their stress, be more likely to sustain their leadership, be more successful, and experience a more satisfying life. Additionally, increased attentiveness to the emotions of staff members facilitates cooperation and can decrease the stress level of everyone in the school (Beatty, 2006).

Successful Principals Take Steps to Stay Healthy

"If you are a person who needs to finish everything every day, the principalship might not be the right job for you."

Reasonable schedule	• "Don't be a martyr."
Good organization	• "Begin the day with priorities."
Flexibility	• "Be able to walk away from the list you never looked at today."
Delegation	• "Share the work load and the leadership with others."
Deflect criticism	• "Pretend there is a glass wall in front of you deflecting criticism."
Sense of humor	• "Without it I'd be drinking on the corner."
Prayer	• "Prayer is woven into my daily life; I ask for guidance to do the right thing."
Connect with peers	• "You will leave thinking, WOW, things are great at my school."

WHAT WORKS IN PRACTICE

Principals shared strategies they used to maintain a healthy perspective about their job. Strategies included dealing with the workload, minimizing stress, handling criticism, sharing with peers, and nurturing their spiritual development.

Limit Your Day. We can all sit and brag that we stay at school until 6:00 p.m. every day and that we are there on Saturday ... but that's not what's going to make you a healthy administrator. I think it's important to [be] able to walk away from the list that you never even looked at today ... to go home and do whatever it is that you do to get away ...

Sometimes principals are martyrs; we want to brag about how we are working ourselves into the ground. But that's not what it's about. You can't stay healthy that way and take care of yourselves, school, and families. You have to balance that and know that every day is a new day. There will be more time to finish [your work]; not everything is urgent.

Get Organized. Being organized is essential—personally and professionally. My family lives and dies by the calendar. We have to. It's the same thing at school.

[Without organization] you would miss a lot. But, having flexibility is important also.

Principals whose time is well-organized and who maintain clean, neat, and attractive offices thereby inspire confidence in their leadership ability.

Nurture Yourself. Take time to nurture your own spirituality. You have to be in touch with what your needs are. We need to present a balanced perspective to students and families. I think that is very important. If you are going to lead a school you have to take that very seriously.

Share With Peers. We really appreciate the opportunity to talk with each other. Unless you phone someone we don't get to talk with each other.

Find time to get together with peers to let down and share. We are all in the same boat so we can all commiserate together. Let it out, understand; then go back with a healthy attitude, a new *can-do* attitude. For me, it is extremely valuable to sit down with my peers and take those deep breaths, and know that I am not the only one that's out there dealing with this.

[The principalship] is a really isolating job. … When we get together, sometimes you walk away feeling like things are pretty good [where you are]. You hear somebody else's problems and appreciate that you aren't experiencing that right now.

During conversations with groups of principals, they told humorous stories about themselves, laughed about their own personality quirks, and joked about mistakes they had made. They entreated staff to do the same:

Laugh. I often remind my office staff, "You've just got to laugh. Go back in the office and have a good laugh." [We are dealing with] children who are learning. [When they] fall off track, you have to dust them off and put them back on; that's what our job is. And isn't that precious!

Some of our [challenges] include adults who are learning, and parents who are learning, and administrators who are learning … you just have to laugh about it.

Think of Mistakes as Opportunities to Learn. Reflect on previous experiences [to learn] what worked or didn't work. Learn from your experiences, professional growth opportunities, and your mistakes. If you don't use your mistakes to learn, you are missing a valuable opportunity.

TAKE ACTION

1. When you know you are working too many hours, take charge of your calendar.

2. When you know your relationships are eroding, revisit your priorities. Jobs come and go; family relationships last forever; friendships are priceless.

3. Organize your calendar; establish a routine; plan your day.

4. Establish a "quitting" time for your day. If you don't finish everything on your "to do" list, add those items to the next day's list.

5. When you go home, be home; leave your work.

6. Nourish yourself; do something "just for you" each day.

7. Be honest about how you feel. Reflect on your feelings and share them with a trusted peer. Keep a journal.

8. Ask staff members how they feel about school issues. Acknowledge their feelings.

9. Create a plan of action to recapture your work-life balance.

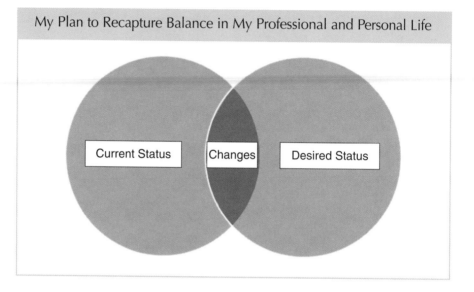

My Plan to Recapture Balance in My Professional and Personal Life

Current Status | Changes | Desired Status

Questions for Reflection

- How long do you work each day? How much time do you spend working on weekends? How can you use your time more efficiently?
- Have you worked with a leader who was well-organized? What organizational strategies did the person use? What do you need to do to become more organized?
- What kinds of emotions do you experience at work? How do you handle those emotions?
- How do you nurture yourself spiritually?
- With whom do you share your emotions, discuss problems at work? Do you have a peer group with whom you can talk honestly about how you feel?
- How do you respond to mistakes?
- When is the last time you laughed at work?

Part II

Operational

Operational practices are the foundation for teaching and learning. Successful schools operate smoothly and seamlessly based on underlying structures. Procedures and policies are in place, environments are healthy and safe, resources and materials are available and adequate, and the right people are on the job.

Often viewed as the mundane part of a principal's role, the daily operational aspects of running a school are critical. These are the conditions that make it possible for teachers to teach and students to learn. Principals who inherit buildings that are unsafe, unhealthy, where students are out of control, and resources are inadequate must first attend to these issues before they can become instructional leaders.

The principals we interviewed described the importance of operational structures such as procedures, environment, resources, and staffing. Some noted the need for operational and organizational change when they moved to new schools.

Tip 7

Fan the Flames of Positive Deviance

Somewhere in your organization, groups of people are already doing things differently and better. To create lasting change, find these areas of positive deviance and fan their flames.

—Pascale and Sternin, 2005, p. 72

- Be alert to school needs.
- Make changes from the inside out.
- Support the innovators in your school.
- Make learning for *all* students the goal.
- Base decisions on a broad base of data.
- Follow the school's mission statement.
- Support change with resources.

Successful principals seize opportunities that benefit all students. They engage in continuous data-based inquiry, analyzing the differences between school vision and reality. They acknowledge deficits and seek improvements. They are solutions oriented and alert to those who do things differently and successfully. Changes are standards-based and consistent with the mission of the school.

These principals look outside the box for answers. They are willing to take risks and try unorthodox solutions if they believe they will result in success for each student. In the words of one principal, "You do whatever it takes."

Their keen perceptions of the school climate and the political tenor of the larger community play a role in the timing and support they generate for innovation and change. They acknowledge that timing is a delicate art, acquired and refined with time and experience. One principal admitted, "There were changes I made too fast during my early years as a principal. These are lessons we learn with practice."

Successful principals know that sustained change must be collaborative. They facilitate change by helping the group understand the problem and fostering broad participation in the change process. Staff members and the school community embrace change because they believe in the change and are invested in the process. They often believe the change was their idea in the first place. Successful principals ensure lasting change by supporting the process with resources including time, training, and funding.

When innovations fail, principals take responsibility for the failure. They examine the causes of the failure to learn from the experience. Once they have completed this process, they can try a new approach to the innovation based on this information.

WHAT THE RESEARCH SAYS

Go to the people. . . . Learn from them. . . . Start with what they know. Build with what they have. . . . When the work is done, the task accomplished, the people will say, "We have done this ourselves."

—Lao-tzu

Decades of research tell us that managing school change is one of the most important tasks of the principalship. Since organizational change demands individual change, it is a critical aspect of successful leadership.

We know that major school initiatives may fail or produce temporary or mediocre results. Fullan (1993a) noted, "We have been fighting an ultimately fruitless uphill battle. The solution is not how to climb the hill of getting more innovations or reforms. ... We need ... a different hill ... a new mindset about educational change" (p. 3). To make and sustain improvements, teachers and administrators must develop new perspectives and become skilled agents of change. Fullan (1992) stated that the focus of change must be on the larger social order, the creation of learning communities and partnerships among agencies.

The following reasons for failure, outlined in Kotter's 1996 book, *Leading Change*, are still noteworthy. They include

- Not establishing a sense of urgency (motivating others to feel the urgency you do). It is difficult to move people out of their comfort zones. Unless the leader can convince the majority of followers that the status quo is unacceptable, the change process is jeopardized before it gets off the ground.

- Not creating a powerful coalition of supporters. The size of the critical mass depends upon the size of the school and the influence of the supporters. A handful of powerful leaders in a small school can lead a major change, while a large school requires supporters whose influence spreads throughout the organization. Kotter cautions that efforts without strong coalitions can make short-term progress; but once the opposition gathers force, they will block the change.

- Lacking a vision that transcends the five-year plan. The vision is a picture of the future that provides direction for the organization. There must be a clear and compelling statement of the vision—one that is easily communicated and readily understood.

- Undercommunicating the vision or behaving in ways that are antithetical to its message. The vision needs to be lived and incorporated into routine messages and discussions so everyone understands how all decisions, changes, and individual performance fit into the larger picture.

- Not removing obstacles to the new vision. Obstacles can include an organizational structure that stifles teacher autonomy and leadership, performance appraisals that do not reward the vision, and lack of resources needed to make desired changes. Sometimes obstacles are negative people whose behavior is allowed to continue unchecked.

- Not systematically planning and creating short-term wins. Maintain enthusiasm by finding ways to demonstrate that gains are being achieved. Celebrate small successes on the way to achieving the larger goal.

- Declaring victory prematurely. If victory is announced too early, old habits creep into practice and progress erodes. Enduring change takes time to become assimilated into school culture. Celebrate small successes while working toward sustained improvement—a process that can require several years.

- Not anchoring change into the culture. The change will be permanent only after it becomes rooted in school norms, is universally valued by existing staff, and is included in the criteria for hiring and inducting new staff. (Kotter, 2009)

Change is a messy, complex process, complicated by barriers, and often accompanied by resistance and confusion. Change is difficult for most people. The loss of the familiar creates unease, even fear. Bacal (2010b) contends that people experience stages of grief, similar to those experienced when a loved one is lost: (1) denial (this will pass); (2) anger and resistance (when they realize the change is here to stay); (3) exploration and acceptance (willing to explore new horizons and accept the change); and (4) commitment (willing to make it work). People adapt to change over extended periods of time. Successful change agents know the importance of anticipating a period of adjustment and are patient as people assimilate the change.

School change requires a visionary leader who understands the change process, can overcome barriers, and can deal with discord (Fullan, 1993a; Stellar, 1988). Additionally, successful change requires that staff members agree that a problem exists and share a sense of urgency to find a solution (Hall & Hord, 1987). Individuals who are required to implement the change mandated by legislation must understand the rationale, be committed to the new procedures (Fullan, 1997), and understand how the change initiative is integral to and interrelated with other aspects of the school (Curtis & Stollar, 2002; Senge, Kleiner, Roberts, Ross, & Smith, 1994). Key factors in the change process include

- You cannot mandate what matters. Complex change cannot be forced.
- Change is a journey rather than a blueprint. It is nonlinear and uncertain.
- Problems are our friends. They are inevitable. Use them to learn.
- Premature visions and planning sometimes blind us to what is needed.
- There are no one-sided solutions.
- Top down and bottom up strategies are both necessary.
- Connections with the wider community are important.
- Every person is a change agent. (Fullan, 1993a, pp. 21–22)

Fullan further explains,

There is a pattern underlying the eight lessons of dynamic change and it concerns one's ability to work with polar opposites: simultaneously pushing for change while allowing self-learning to unfold; being prepared for a journey of uncertainty; seeing problems as sources of creative resolution; having a vision, but not being blinded by it; valuing the individual and the group; incorporating centralizing and decentralizing forces; being internally cohesive, but externally oriented; and valuing personal change agentry as the route to system change. (Fullan, 1993a, p. 40)

Steps in the change process include establishing or understanding the educational vision or mission of the school, assessing progress toward school goals, identifying areas for improvement, developing solutions, and implementing changes effectively (North Central Regional Educational Laboratory, 1995). Sergiovanni (2009) outlines a useful procedure for change agents:

- Clarify the school's mission in light of reasons for change. Consider whether or not the change is possible, needed, or useful.
- Establish roles, responsibilities, and structure to support the change. Identify leaders and develop cohesiveness and skills to support the process.
- Develop leadership team capability, skills, and support.
- Objectively appraise the current situation.
- Determine the strategies required for change.
- Develop implementation plans that include support mechanisms, such as communication systems, and training, measurement, and monitoring systems.
- Celebrate, reflect, and document learning for the next change event.

Pascale and Sternin (2005) contend that in every organization there are isolated groups and individuals who are successful in spite of prevailing obstacles and barriers. Their practices can become indigenous models of change when mainstreamed into the organization. Doing so requires a departure from the traditional and more comfortable use of benchmarks and best practices, which rely on copying an external authority. Pascale and Sternin suggest that the key to change is to engage members of the organization in a process of discovery, inviting the community to identify solutions and spearhead change. Leaders relinquish their role of expert and chief decision maker and engage in discovery with the group. Pascale and Sternin (2005) developed the following six-step model of positive deviance.

1. Make the group the guru: Problem identification, ownership, and action begin in and remain in the group.

2. Reframe the facts: Restate the problem to focus attention on exceptions to the norm, evidence of instances where others overcame this problem.

3. Make it safe to learn: Problems go unresolved if people fear ridicule, retaliation, or loss.

4. Make the problem concrete: Name the problem so the meaning is not lost in obscurity.

5. Leverage social proof: Identify and share examples of success.

6. Confound the immune defense response: Avoid resistance by fanning embers of change within the community rather than using heavy-handed authority.

WHAT WORKS IN PRACTICE

According to the principals interviewed, making changes that advanced school improvement was a major component of their job. Regardless of the issue at hand, timing, gathering input, analyzing data, planning, taking calculated risks, and admitting mistakes were factors included in the change process. A high school principal explained, "The whole change thing is really a balancing act. You don't want to be this maverick jumping on every band-wagon … but you don't want to be the turtle swimming through the mud either. There has to be a balance."

Principals agreed that major changes needed to be based on data gathered from multiple sources. Stakeholders should be involved in the change process as well. All of the principals mentioned the importance of getting out of the office to know what is happening in the building.

I don't know that you could make a decision for change without input from other people—teachers, parents, students, your supervisor, or pastor. Most decisions require input, collaboration, and feedback.

I am not comfortable being the one who makes changes that everyone else has to live by. I formed a leadership team with representatives from grade levels and special areas that meets quarterly to talk about the lay of the land and what needs to happen. We discuss everything; grade level dynamics, children who need special attention, curriculum issues, and other topics. It would be ridiculous for any leader to look at the faces of qualified and highly motivated staff and say, "I'm going to do it my way." Once we make decisions together, my staff [members] are my allies; it's partly their decision so there is ownership.

Look at the data; examine what's going well. Look at anecdotal and hard data from a lot of sources; brainstorm, look at needs, and decide where you need to go. Start planning. Bear in mind your overall mission and school goals as you plan.

Principals agreed that calculated risk taking was part of change. An elementary principal explained,

If you don't take risks, you will continue doing the same old things. Sometimes your idea works; sometimes it fails. If it doesn't work, just say, I do not think that was the right decision. I don't think that it is bad to show that you can make mistakes like everyone else. [Teachers] will forgive you if you are honest in admitting mistakes—*just don't do it too often.*

Principals sought feedback from parents on school performance and when considering new directions. Some formed parent boards; one of them used town hall meetings. The principal who reported using town hall meetings said they yielded valuable information about what was working and what new directions needed to be taken. She cautioned about the importance of selecting a skilled facilitator to lead the meeting—that it needed to be someone who could keep conversations positive and focused on the topic at hand.

I have a parent board with whom I share the inside scoop of what's happening in the school and why decisions were made. I gather their feedback and learn what directions will best benefit families.

Following is an example of a principal who was unwilling to accept the status quo:

Mr. M. is a principal of an elementary school in a rural African village. His students are lively, smiling, and learning in spite of living in impoverished conditions. Some of the students have AIDS; many of them are orphans of parents who died of AIDS. They live with relatives who have barely enough food for their families, much less food for another child. They own few articles of clothing; most of them have no shoes.

When Mr. M. took the job, he inherited a school consisting of three ramshackle tin structures housing a few tables and benches, no running water, no electricity, with a curricula printed on large sheets of paper taped to the walls. At noon, village women prepared tea under a tree for children who were fortunate enough to own a cup. There was no food.

Mr. M. knew that some of the children would not receive an evening meal. Since hungry children cannot learn, he made securing food his first priority. He enlisted the support of the school staff, and a few volunteers, and began a school garden. He and his staff planted a garden, watering it with buckets of water carried over rough terrain from a river located a half mile away. Everything they grew was sent home with students.

Eventually, he hopes that the volunteers will make this a village project. In the meantime, he and his staff maintain their garden, richly rewarded by the smiles of children—no longer hungry and eager to learn.

TAKE ACTION

Making School Improvements

1. What problem do you want to address?
2. What data support the need for the change?
3. What changes will solve the problem?
4. Who will lead the change?
5. What roles can the leadership team assume?
6. How will you motivate them?
7. How would the change support the vision and mission of the school?
8. How does the change support curriculum standards?

9. What barriers and constraints exist?

10. Who will oppose the change?

11. What education or training is needed to create a cohesive leadership team?

12. What education or training is needed for staff members?

13. How will you implement the change?

14. How will you monitor and evaluate success?

15. How will you celebrate small successes?

16. How will you ensure that the change becomes part of the school culture?

Questions for Reflection

- Although conditions in your school are probably not as extreme as those of Mr. M., most schools have status quo situations that need to be examined. Consider the conditions and situations in the school that have been accepted as "the ways things are." Should any of these situations be reevaluated, challenged, changed? Be aware that if the situation is entrenched in school culture, making change will upset some individuals. Who would be upset with a change in status quo? Who would welcome a change? How can you help people identify the situation as a problem that needs to be changed? What evidence of success can you find elsewhere? How should you begin?

- What obvious changes are needed in your school? What data do you have that supports the need and the potential solution? How can you engage the staff in identifying the problem and supporting change? How should you begin?

- What is the teachers' vision for the future? What positive and realistic changes do they believe would improve student learning?

- What conditions outside the school are interfering with student learning? Is it possible for the school to improve any of these conditions? If so, what solutions might be possible? Who or what agencies could assist you?

- What lessons have you learned from previous experiences with school change? What worked well in the past? What differences in this school or situation need to be considered? What previous mistakes do you want to avoid?

Tip 8

Improve Education From the Inside: Empower Teachers

The teacher who works for or allows the status quo is the traitor.

—Fullan, 1993b, p. 14

Mandates do not create sustained change, teachers do. Teachers are the true holders of power as change agents in education. As teachers of the future citizenry, Fullan (1993b) reminds us that teachers are the moral change agents in society. Their values and beliefs about teaching and learning permeate what they teach, the methods they use, and their behavior with students. If we want to change schools and learning, we must begin with teachers. When teachers decide change is needed, it will happen, and it will be sustainable.

Most teachers begin their careers with the moral impetus to make a difference. However, teachers may be treated like workers, not leaders. If little attention is paid to their ideas for improving education, if little attention is given to the core values, philosophy, and vision that motivate them to act, then they may adopt the attitude of the worker bee who tolerates or complains about what is rather than seeking what could be. Seeing little relevance or benefit to changes that come and go, they close their door and continue to teach as they always have. Meanwhile, frustrated officials are baffled about the failure of educational reform efforts.

Teachers are in a position to become powerful catalysts for change. However, we must first engage them in seeking change that they perceive as important for their students. Just as a leader's personal belief system underlies personal leadership style, a teacher's philosophy of teaching and learning influences teaching behavior—what happens when the classroom door is closed.

Teachers need to periodically reexamine their personal vision. Fullan contends, "Paradoxically, personal purpose is the route to organizational change" (1993b, p. 3). Engaging teachers in a dialogue about their values, beliefs, and vision for the future of education can rekindle enthusiasm and imagination, and prompt them to become proactive change agents for education. Enduring change occurs, from the inside out.

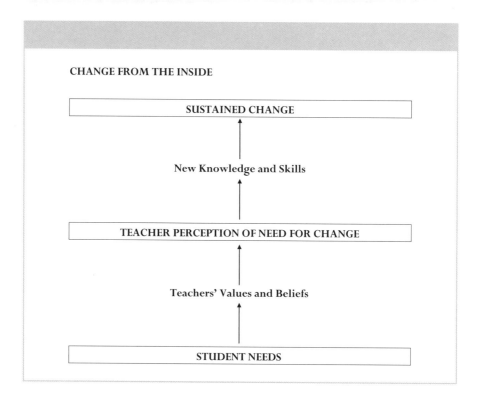

CHANGE FROM THE INSIDE

SUSTAINED CHANGE

↑

New Knowledge and Skills

↑

TEACHER PERCEPTION OF NEED FOR CHANGE

↑

Teachers' Values and Beliefs

↑

STUDENT NEEDS

WHAT THE RESEARCH SAYS

The concept of teachers as change agents is not a new one. Researchers were promoting the notion of teachers as change agents three decades ago. Nickse (1973) stated teachers should assume leadership roles, arguing that their direct link to student learning, knowledge of the school system, and vested interest placed them in the optimal position. Factors that prevented their assuming leadership included their self-perception as teacher-workers, fear of reprisal, and lack of support from administrators.

Fullan (1993b) reported, "Moral purpose and change agentry are implicit in what good teaching and effective change are about, but as yet they are society's (and teaching's) great untapped resources for radical and continuous improvement" (p. 11). Teachers begin their careers with a sense of moral purpose; they believe they have the ability to make a difference through teaching. Moral purpose, or making a difference, involves change. Teachers are motivated to change if they believe the change directly benefits students. By virtue of their moral purpose, teachers are natural change agents. However, one need only look at the high attrition rate of teachers to realize that many teachers are never invited to fulfill their commitment (Ingersoll, 2003).

Instead, they take their talents to other careers. Other promising teachers succumb to burnout, never fulfilling their true potential (Farber, 1991; Brock & Grady, 2002). Fullan (1993b) suggested a new paradigm that synthesized the moral purpose of teachers with their powerful potential as change agents.

To become innovative change agents, teachers need to periodically reexamine what they believe, what their students need, and how best to fulfill those needs. Without periodic reexamination and recommitment to personal beliefs, teachers quickly become absorbed into an existing school culture without questioning its effectiveness, much less initiating change. They participate in groupthink, reacting to what is rather than seeking what can be. Morrison (1966) reminded us, "People become culture bound, tied to a set of feelings; fixed attitudes. It's human" (p. 122).

Fullan (1993b) suggested that personal vision emerges from within, giving meaning to work, and existing independently from the organization. When teachers reexamine and articulate their personal vision, kindred spirits and shared ideas emerge within the group. Groupthink is replaced with new ideas that challenge the status quo. The stage is set for teachers to create a new vision for the school and make changes for the benefit of students. When teachers decide that change is needed, their potential to create sustained change that redesigns education is profound.

One's personal vision evolves and changes as new knowledge and experience are acquired and integrated with core values. Van Driel, Beijaard, and Verloop (2000) note school improvement efforts are often unsuccessful because they fail to consider teachers' existing knowledge, beliefs, and attitudes. They argue that teachers construct practical knowledge by integrating experiential knowledge, formal knowledge, and personal beliefs. Since teachers' classroom practices flow from an integrated set of beliefs and knowledge, professional development programs are needed to achieve sustained school change (Van Driel et al., 2000). Teachers' practical knowledge (Duffee & Aikenhead, 1992) and belief systems (Tobin & McRobbie, 1996) exert a profound influence on the way they respond to change. School reformers who ignore teachers' existing knowledge and belief systems are unlikely to succeed.

WHAT WORKS IN PRACTICE

Principals we met seized opportunities to engage in conversation with teachers about values and beliefs regarding teaching and learning. Suggestions included

- Use discussion of values as a foundation for the formation of learning communities.
- Include discussion of values and beliefs into established staff development programs.
- Use case studies to engage teachers in a discussion of values and beliefs.
- Buy teachers a thought-provoking book for summer reading and engage teachers in discussions about the book in the fall to stimulate dialogue about values.
- Have teachers take the Gallup *Strengths Finder* (Rath, 2007) and engage them in a discussion of their individual strengths and how those strengths and preferences guide their interactions with each other and decisions about teaching practices.

TAKE ACTION

My role, as I saw it, was to promote thinking, among adults as well as children.

—Villani, 2008, p. 48

Challenge teachers to examine and articulate their core values and personal vision. Engage teachers in an examination of their assumptions about teaching and their reasons for being teachers. Most teachers enter the profession for a reason and with a desire to make a difference. Over the years, however, daily teaching and groupthink that permeates a school may obscure purpose and ideals. Individual goals can be overshadowed by imposed roles and the expectations of others. Unless teachers periodically reexamine their values and renew personal goals, the realization of goals is unlikely. Articulating the reasons they entered teaching, their vision for teaching and learning, and their hopes for the future is reenergizing and a prerequisite for sustained change.

Before holding a discussion session, give teachers a couple of days to reflect on two simple questions: "Why did I go into teaching?" and "What difference am I trying to make?" Organize discussion sessions into groups of five and ask one teacher in each group to moderate the discussion so everyone has an opportunity to share. Use the responses of participants to determine what questions to include in later discussions. The list of values in the Appendix might assist teachers as they consider their values. Use the following list to get started:

- Why did I go into teaching?
- What difference do I want to make?
- What is the purpose of teaching?
- What should students learn in school?
- What is the role of a teacher?
- What is my vision for the future of education/the school/the students?
- How do my goals fit those of the school?
- What changes can I make in my classroom/the school/the district to promote that vision?

Since expertise is central to the ability to change, once teachers decide on a new direction, they need to consider what new skills or practices must be acquired. Vision is a starting point; knowledge and skill are required to bring vision to fruition. When teachers have concluded a discussion of personal vision, engage them in a discussion of the skills and practices required to make their vision a reality.

- How have needs of students changed?
- What advancements in knowledge and teaching skills will meet student needs?
- What are my strengths? How can I best use them?
- What new skills do I need to master?
- What new practices should I use?
- How can I acquire these skills?

Redirect the conversation from the individual to the faculty as a group.

- How can we use our individual strengths to collaborate?
- How do our personal goals mesh with school goals?
- What are the needs of students in our school?
- What can we do as a faculty to improve the education of all students in the school?
- What changes do we need to make?
- What skills do we need to learn?
- What can be gained from collaboration?
- How should we structure our time to provide for collaboration?

Questions for Reflection

- How do I feel about the notion that teachers are the true holders of power as school change agents?
- When considering change, do I begin with the teachers by soliciting their ideas and input?
- If asked, would teachers in my building say they are treated like worker bees or leaders?
- When did I last have a conversation with teachers about their personal vision of teaching and learning?
- Do teachers in my school feel comfortable enough to suggest a change? Or do they hesitate out of fear of reprisal?
- When was the last time a teacher suggested a change? What was the outcome of that suggestion?

Tip 9

Hire the Best and Maximize Their Talents

A principal's job is to visit classrooms to see if the children are learning.

—John, age 10

- Hire the best.
- Hire people who have talents you do not have.
- Put the right people in the right places.
- Give them a good start.
- Develop their potential.
- If they don't want to go in the direction you are going … get them off the bus.

Successful principals know that the success of the school depends on the effectiveness of the school staff. They use their position, power, and influence to hire the best people, place them where their talents are most suited, and develop their gifts to the fullest. They offer opportunities to grow and change. To do this, they need to know what is happening in the school, what is working, and where changes need to occur. Sometimes the right teachers are in the school, but their talents are underutilized in the grade level or area they are teaching. To bring out the best in teachers and staff, they need to be working in a situation that optimizes their abilities. Principals need to be visibly and actively engaged with teachers, office staff, cafeteria workers, and maintenance staff. Everyone's talents are valuable; everyone's voice is important.

Although principals usually do not have the luxury of selecting the entire school staff, they do select and induct replacement staff, transfer teachers to other schools as appropriate, and supervise and coach the entire school staff. Each of these tasks presents an opportunity for school improvement.

Effective school leaders recognize the importance of hiring decisions and selection of staff members whose knowledge, skills, and dispositions are the "right fit" for the school. The performance of new staff members contributes to school success. The principals we talked with were mission driven in fulfilling staffing needs. They emphasized the following attributes in their hiring decisions:

1. Able to fulfill mission of the school

2. Able to fulfill existing curriculum needs

3. Complemented talents of existing staff

4. Student centered in approach to teaching

5. Innovative, self-starter

6. Able to collaborate with others

The talents of newly hired staff members are cultivated and shaped through participation in a meaningful and extensive induction process.

Successful principals seize opportunities to raise expectations and performance levels of everyone who works in the school. They visit classrooms, hallways, and gathering places, offering help to teachers, and listening to students. Teachers welcome their presence, knowing that the feedback, recommendations, and encouragement they receive are based on knowledge and experience. Because principals visit the classrooms, they can spot teachers who have lost their passion for teaching or are dissatisfied with the school. Everyone's interests are served when principals counsel disenchanted teachers into more suitable occupations or arrange transfers to more appropriate school settings.

Successful principals are visible and involved. They use their influence to promote excellence by modeling and rewarding excellent performance. Mindful of the adage, "We do what is rewarded," principals praise teachers whose performance leads to student learning, collegiality, and the attainment of school goals. They refuse to accept mediocrity, negativity, and "difficult" behaviors, aware that left unchecked, these behaviors become the norm.

When principals identify a teacher who would benefit from a change of scenery or the stimulation of a new grade level or assignment, they suggest a change. Complacency, disenchantment, and burnout creep up slowly; teachers may be unaware of the symptoms and therefore, object to a change. A skillful principal can present the change as a positive opportunity. Even if the change is initially unwelcome, most teachers come to realize the benefits of the change.

WHAT THE RESEARCH SAYS

Effective school leaders hire talented teachers and provide opportunities and autonomy to use their talents. Using the analogy suggested by Collins (2001), put the right people on the bus and in the right seats. Given the opportunity to participate in hiring decisions, seek teachers who are self-disciplined, knowledgeable, organized, and have superior people skills. Look for teachers who are self-starters; those who will welcome new challenges and who are willing to persevere when the going gets tough. Look for teachers who are potential leaders. Weak principals can be threatened by teachers who are self-starters, that is, teachers who might challenge their ideas (Streich, 2009). Sometimes, teacher leaders are mistakenly labeled as "difficult" because they rock the boat by questioning decisions and suggesting new ideas. Effective leaders recognize these "caged eagles" and find opportunities to use their leadership abilities (Brock & Grady, 2009).

Although hiring the most talented teachers is the first step, the success of teachers requires a quality induction program followed by career-long staff development. New teachers require time and assistance to become master teachers. Experienced teachers require renewal and development to enhance their skills. Successful principals realize time and effort spent socializing new teachers into the school culture and continued professional development is a long-term investment in student learning and school success (Brock & Grady, 2007).

The induction period becomes the first phase of professional development that includes formative supervision and new skill acquisition. Successful principals view classroom visits as an opportunity to facilitate excellence in teaching by offering suggestions, encouraging perseverance, and affirming stellar performance rather than engaging in fault-finding missions (Streich, 2009). Although supervisory measures may differ according to school system and personal style, successful principals know what is being taught and what is happening throughout their school; teachers view them as collaborators in the instructional and curricular process (Glickman, Gordon, & Ross-Gordon, 2010). Additionally, they recognize that teachers, like students, need the motivating experience of success along the way (Henson, 2010), an experience that requires more than an obligatory supervisory visit and a meaningless rating sheet.

Although successful principals develop teachers by building on strengths, they are quick to point out and curtail behaviors that adversely affect or threaten school goals and the instructional process. They are aware of the destructive nature of difficult behaviors and take prompt action to curtail them before they interfere with school goals, diminish school climate, and interfere with student learning. Their prompt action sends a clear message that inappropriate behavior (such as persistent negativity, constant complaining, malicious gossiping, criticizing students and parents) is not acceptable and will not be tolerated. Leaders who are aware, but ignore, the behavior of difficult individuals, send a message that the behavior will be tolerated, a choice that lowers their leadership credibility among school staff. They run the additional risk of toxic subcultures developing among staff members (Brock & Grady, 2009).

WHAT WORKS IN PRACTICE

Teachers had strong feelings about the importance of having the right teachers in the right places:

> I believe that if a teacher does not move in a direction that is beneficial to students, the principal must help the teacher see that he or she is not a good fit for the building.

> There are two teachers in my school who were once good teachers, but who have become jaded and cynical. My principal must have noticed it also because he is moving them to different grade levels. They are not happy about it. Personally, I think once they get involved in learning new materials and move to new classrooms they will become reinvigorated— excited about teaching again. He is taking a lot of criticism for it, but I admire him.

> It's about having high expectations. Successful principals raise the bar. The principal sets the tone for the building, and makes sure the best people are doing the right jobs. When everyone in the school sees that the principal puts students first, and every decision is made with the thought, "Is this what is best for kids," it becomes a schoolwide expectation.

Principals need to make sure that teachers have a true sense of their strengths and weaknesses, then help them grow by playing to their strengths and working with them to continue growth in a weak area. You might not be able to make a mediocre teacher great, but you can make the person better.

Principals shared their practices:

I think it is essential to be visible and stay involved. Students and teachers want and expect to see the principal in their classrooms. The principal's presence informs students and teachers that they are important and that learning is the primary business of the school. Principals who stay in their office is one of the main complaints of teachers.

Get out of your office. I write it on my agenda for the day to remind myself to get out and do it.

Be a visible presence: Walk through the school, visit classrooms, talk with teachers, students, and parents to better understand the people that make up the school.

I spend a lot of time in classrooms so I keep a pager on me so [office staff] know where to find me. I spend a huge amount of time in classrooms. I make it a point to visit with teachers, stop by classrooms. I don't want them to feel I am checking up on them. It's just a matter of asking, "How's it going?"

I make a point to visit the cafeteria and playground, but I am not on the roster for duty. I visit. I hit the ball with the kids, but I am not the person responsible every day because I cannot guarantee that I will be available. I need to be able to walk away if I need to.

> When I leave my door open, it's like Grand Central Station with "Do you have a minute?" or " Sorry to interrupt you, but …" I find that days when I am right there, I have a lot of contact because teachers can find me. When I am not in my office—out and about the building visiting classrooms, I hear, "You weren't there. I looked for you all morning and wanted to talk to you about …" and then it's a criticism. "You were not available when I needed you." It is a challenge to find a balance.

> You have to find a time when you can be available to teachers because they are busy throughout the day. It's a balancing act.

> The days I eat my lunch in my office, teachers stop to visit; that's when they are free and try to find me.

Ms. B. is one example of an exemplary principal known for her ability to hire and develop talented teachers. She was head of an elementary school with a high population of impoverished, transient, and homeless families. She needed to maintain a school staff equipped to deal with the issues of homeless students and ever-changing class enrollments and was keenly aware that despite good intentions, not all teachers were emotionally equipped to deal with the realities and ramifications of extreme poverty and homelessness.

During the hiring process and induction period, she was clear about the needs of the school population and her expectations for performance. She told all newly hired teachers,

> We are here to serve the students and families who make up this school population. We love our students and we provide many community services at this school to assist them and their families. We do not engage in negative comments about students or criticisms of parents. Instead, we look for proactive solutions to foster student learning and assist their families, many of whom are facing challenging circumstances.
>
> If, at any time, you discover that you cannot love these children, deal with the issues they present, and make their families feel welcomed and respected, please tell me. I understand that this is not the right school for all teachers, and if you need a change, I will help you find a school that is a better match for the gifts you bring to teaching.

TAKE ACTION

1. Who needs a change on your staff? What are your reasons for seeking this change? Where would the person's talents be better utilized?

2. How will you approach this change with the teacher? What problems do you anticipate? What district policies do you need to follow? What union constraints exist?

3. Who would enjoy a new challenge? Is it possible to facilitate a change, a move, or provide a new experience?

Questions for Reflection

- What strategies do you use to select teachers who are the "right fit" for your school? Do you need to reconsider the interview process?
- What strategies do you use to identify and develop the strengths of teachers?
- What do you do when you notice a good teacher losing enthusiasm?
- How do you decide when to change a teacher's placement or teaching assignment?
- What process do you use to encourage or counsel a teacher into a new assignment?
- How do you handle unhappy teachers and staff criticism when you have made an unpopular change of assignment?
- How do you use teachers' successes to motivate their continued improvement?
- How often are you seen in classrooms?
- How often do you have conversations with teachers about their teaching, the curriculum, or ways in which you can assist them?
- If asked, what would students say about your knowledge and concern for what happens in their classes? What evidence would they offer?
- What would teachers say about your knowledge and concern for what happens in their classes? What evidence would they offer?

Tip 10

Use a Team Approach: Think "We" Instead of "I"

The leaders who work most effectively, it seems to me, never say "I." And that's not because they have trained themselves not to say "I." They don't think "I." They think "we"; they think "team." They understand their job to be to make the team function. They accept responsibility and don't sidestep it, but "we" gets the credit. This is what creates trust, what enables you to get the task done.

—Peter Drucker

- Think in terms of "WE" not "I."
- Staff the team with the right people.
- Provide a framework of expectations and accountability.
- Offer training and assistance where needed.
- Allow autonomy in delivering results.
- Give credit to the team for successes.
- Accept responsibility for failure.

Andrew Carnegie said, "Teamwork is the fuel that allows common people to attain uncommon results. One mind plus a second mind equals a third mind and the possibility to create new ideas and better solutions more quickly" (Hutchings, 2009). Successful principals achieve uncommon results through teamwork that operates within and beyond the school. They create a powerful synergy (derived from a Greek word meaning "coming together") by meshing the diversified expertise and talents of staff and parents, resulting in greater advances in student learning. People within the school community feel united in a common cause and are willing to extend themselves for the greater good. A sense of "we" prevails.

Principals who achieve dynamic teams make it look easy. There is, however, more to teamwork than organizing people into groups and committees, as the principal in the following example discovered.

Mr. Z. is a high school principal who professes a strong belief in teamwork. He has organized several teams of teachers who routinely meet after school and share feedback and findings with him. However, teachers have noticed that Mr. Z. continues to make decisions that appear to disregard their input. None of their suggestions have been implemented. They are beginning to think the team concept exists in name only and resent the valuable time they are using for the meetings. Anger is growing and teachers are no longer willing to attend team meetings. Mr. Z. is perplexed at their response.

In the example, Mr. Z. had the right idea, but failed to clarify the purpose of the team, the scope of its authority, and how feedback would be used. The exercise resulted in angry teachers who perceived Mr. Z's team approach as nothing but a sham. He lost credibility and damaged staff morale.

True teamwork is genuine and based on respect for the team's ability to produce results. Effective teams are staffed with people with adequate experience and expertise to accomplish the task. The goal is worthy of the time extended and identifiably related to instruction and student learning. Each team needs a predetermined goal, an organizational structure, a measure of accountability, time and resources to accomplish the task, and a clear understanding of how findings will be used. Once in motion, teams require a measure of autonomy. At the end of the journey, team members need to be recognized for their contribution and the information or decision used in accordance with the original plan. If a new initiative fails, however, the administrator needs to accept responsibility.

WHAT THE RESEARCH SAYS

Extensive studies extol the benefits of teamwork. School communities that share a common vision for the school and operate from a collective responsibility for student learning are more successful in developing school programs that improve student learning (Bryk & Driscoll, 1985; Glickman et al., 2010; Newmann & Wehlage, 1995). Additionally, we know that school leadership is second only to teaching as an influence on student learning and when leadership is distributed it is more effective (Leithwood, Harris, & Hopkins, 2008). Research indicates the leadership of the principal is the critical factor in creating conditions in which teamwork and student learning thrive (Hallinger & Heck, 1996; Rosenholtz, 1989). Anecdotal reports of veteran principals warn that failure to collaborate is an invitation for failure. According to Young (2006), "If you allow yourself to go too far out on a limb alone, you can expect others to saw it off behind you" (p. 20).

Generational Differences. Since a typical school staff includes teachers whose ages range from early 20s to late 60s, creating teams involves facilitating a cooperative endeavor between different generations of teachers. Awareness of the recent research on generational diversity offers valuable insight into maximizing the potential of teams by balancing them along generational lines (O'Donovan, 2009).

Herley (2009) suggests an examination of the following generations in organizations: (1) Veterans, (2) Baby Boomers, (3) Generation Xers, and (4) Millenials or Generation Y. Since each generation of teachers has had a different life experience, they hold differing views on the needs of students, the nature of teaching and learning, and what constitutes appropriate learning experiences. Their solutions to problems will vary in accordance with their life experiences.

O'Donovan (2009) suggests creating teams that consider generational diversity as well as gender and ethnicity. Today's schools are likely to include staff members from multiple generations. These generations grew up with different events and experiences shaping their lives. Thus, they view the world through different lenses; have differing values, views, ambitions, and skills (Zemke, Raines, & Filipczak, 2000); and may need to be reminded of the thread that unites them: the school's vision and mission. Individuals from each generation, however, want the same basic things: feeling valued, knowing that what they contribute matters, opportunities to learn and grow, a sense of community at work, and to be successful (Burmeister, 2008).

Acknowledged, appreciated, and used, the differences in perspectives and skills can lend value rather than create barriers. Although the skills and attitudes of generations defy defining dates and simple categorization the following summaries may be useful:

1. Veterans (born between 1922 and 1943) are the generation that created the school system as we know it. Although most have retired, a few remain in positions of higher status. The system of education built by this generation was based on a hierarchy that values seniority and the notion of paying one's dues.

2. Baby Boomers (born between 1944 and 1960) value their status as experienced teachers and leaders who formed the basis for current

school culture and practices. They expect that their experience and opinions will be valued during decision making.

3. Generation Xers (born between 1960 and 1980) are experienced with and enjoy teamwork and collaboration. They prefer developing creative options to receiving dictates from superiors.

4. Millennial teachers (born between 1980 and 2000) are just beginning to enter the profession. Since they are inexperienced, they listen to or are ambivalent toward more veteran colleagues. They bring high energy, enthusiasm, technological skills, and recent experience as students to the mix (O'Donovan, 2009).

Regardless of how one defines them, success in school improvement requires the collaboration of the generations. Successful leaders are cognizant of and plan for generational differences that can either facilitate or hinder teamwork. If you suspect, but are not certain, that conflicts have a basis in generational differences, conduct an assessment to learn the underlying causes. Ask questions; listen.

Strategies to foster cooperative teamwork across generations include opportunities for purposeful conversation. People who know each other on a personal level are more likely to cooperate. Engage teachers in dialogue to (1) identify their differences in perspectives and skills, (2) acknowledge the gifts each group brings, and (3) identify strategies that will maximize the gifts that each group brings to the table. Create opportunities for pairs or small groups of teachers of different generations to work together on projects. Pair two teachers from different generations to teach each other something. Plan opportunities for teachers to socialize during school hours. Heeding the words of Plato, "You can discover more about a person in an hour of play than in a year of conversation."

The Skill of the Team Leader. Effective teamwork depends on the skill of the leader. Teamwork can be disastrous unless the leader is skilled in developing and working with a team. Autocratic leaders who micromanage, apply rigid constraints, withhold autonomy, or use elastic autonomy (never constant), create directionless, confused, and ineffective teams. When team members realize the team is a sham and they are wasting their time, they become resentful and angry. The leader loses credibility (Bacal, 2010a).

By contrast, some school leaders become so enamored with the concept of teamwork that every decision becomes a team event, often to the dismay of busy classroom teachers. Using a team approach when the decision does not affect the entire group can be counterproductive and a waste of time. Some decisions and tasks are best left to the discretion of the principal acting alone. Bacal (2010a) cautions against using teamwork to perform tasks when

(1) the task is simple, (2) little communication is required, (3) the information to complete the task is held by one person, (4) components of the task are unrelated, (5) the team approach would needlessly slow progress or reduce productivity, or (6) there is extreme instability within the larger organization.

In summary, we know that successful leadership depends on principals facilitating teams that function cohesively and meet desired goals. What eludes us, however, is *how* principals take a group of diverse people and transform them into a dynamic group.

Part of the answer might lie in what drives principals to create teams in the first place. During our conversations, principals talked about their need to obtain a broad base of input before making decisions. They were humble in admitting they did not have all of the answers. They formed teams with staff members, parents, and students as a mechanism to gather data and solve problems. They knew what kinds of data they needed, asked the right people, and used the data for school improvement. The people in their schools became invested in the solutions and were consequently willing to make Herculean efforts on behalf of student learning. Since teams evolved out of a genuine desire to include people, teams became part of everyday practice rather than token attempts at following a leadership trend. Everyone in the school community has a part.

WHAT WORKS IN PRACTICE

Principals shared their thoughts and strategies:

I am very cautious about being *the one* who makes the decision that everyone else has to live by ... so I formed a leadership team. Even though I have a relatively small staff, I was not comfortable making changes without their input especially since I came from a high school environment, and I really don't know how to teach reading or elementary math. I depended on high-quality teachers at the primary level who could teach me [about those areas] and give me information to make a decision. So I formed the leadership team—one teacher from each level and a teacher representing the special areas. We meet quarterly to talk about the lay of the land, what's happening, the dynamics at their level, curriculum issues, and if there are children that we need to be particularly concerned about. I bring my agenda to the meetings and throw it out for the group to discuss. I feel strongly about my agenda and will pursue it to the extent that they allow me to. But, it would be ridiculous for me, or any leader, to look at the faces of a very qualified, highly motivated staff and say, I'm going to do it anyway. Helping them understand where I am coming from and hearing them is very important. Once we make a decision, they are my allies; it is partly their decision, so there is ownership.

It's all about creating a team. When I went to my last school, there was no place for teachers to sit and talk. That's a different culture than I want to be around. I want teachers talking and sharing ideas. When it comes to change, I don't know that you could make a decision without input from other people—teachers, parents, students, your supervisor. Most decisions should not be made without collaboration. You may have your own agenda, but you bring people along so it's their ideas being discussed. I can't imagine doing it another way.

I have a parent board composed of some very dedicated parents. Since they are willing to meet with me every month, I am comfortable sharing some of the inside scoop of what's [happening in the school.] Doing so generates allegiance, ownership, and a greater understanding of why decisions are being made. I ask for their feedback on how things should be presented, what direction we should go to best benefit families.

We [recently] had a town hall meeting … facilitated by [an expert]. After I presented an informational PowerPoint about the school, I left. He divided everyone into groups and asked them to address these questions: What should [the school] start? What should [the school] continue? What should [the school] stop? And what are your burning questions? [The results] were phenomenal. The dynamics were positive and encouraging, and we gathered many good ideas. We compiled the information and sent it out to all the parents. Each week I take a few points and address them. There is a real chance for this sort of thing to go negative, but the person who was leading it was able to keep that from happening. He was excellent, able to redirect comments about any individual child or individual teachers, to set the stage. I would do it again in a heartbeat.

A teacher shared:

My principal has a Principal's Round Table to gather valuable information from students. He asks questions about issues such as feeling welcome in the building, feeling safe, being bullied, how adults treat them, and questions related to curriculum.

TAKE ACTION

Identify ways you can improve teamwork in your school:

1. In what areas and from whom do you need additional input?
2. What is the purpose of the group?
3. Who should be included in the group?
4. What generational issues might be anticipated?
5. What will you do with the input?
6. How will you assess effectiveness?

SCHOOL GROUPS AND FUNCTIONS

Teaming With Teachers

Area of Need	Group Purpose	Group Membership	Input Use	Assessment Strategy

Teaming With Parents

Area of Need	Group Purpose	Group Membership	Input Use	Assessment Strategy

Teaming With Students

Area of Need	Group Purpose	Group Membership	Input Use	Assessment Strategy

Questions for Reflection

- How do you routinely make important decisions?
- Where, how, and from whom do you obtain data?
- Would teachers say that they are included in decisions that affect them?
- Would they say that a team spirit prevails in the school?
- What is the purpose of the committees or teams that you have established in the school?
- How could they be more effective?
- How many school committees are ineffective, need restructuring, or should be eliminated?
- What mechanism do you use to obtain feedback and input from parents?
- How effective is it?
- Would parents say that their input and feedback is invited?
- Would they say that there is a partnership between parents and the school?
- How often do you talk with students about their perceptions and experiences?

Tip 11

Honor the Role of the Classroom Teachers

Remember what it was like to be a teacher. Long days with no breaks. The lesson that goes great or goes off track. The parent who just doesn't get it. Without that insight into what it is like to be a teacher, it is easy to make decisions that are impractical for the classroom. If you are supportive, teachers are more likely to be supportive of your decisions.

—Elementary principal

- Make sure teachers have the time they need to teach.
- Give them time to plan and collaborate during the school day.
- Support goals with resources.
- Keep the school environment safe and healthful.
- Support teachers' decisions.
- Show your appreciation.

Honor the role of teachers and protect their time to teach. Teachers make learning possible. They are the school's greatest resource and the key to school success. In a job where demands are growing, rewards are diminishing, and criticism is abundant, teachers need principals who champion their efforts.

Teachers spend long hours with students, each of whom presents different abilities, past learning experiences, personalities, work ethics, and family circumstances. They are expected to tailor the learning experience to maximize individual student's success, teach stellar lessons in well-managed classrooms, meet legislated learning benchmarks, attend to student's personal issues, work with families, collaborate with colleagues, participate in professional development, attend after-school events and meetings, plan lessons, grade papers, and handle attendant paper work. Although the demands continue to grow in number, the amount of available time does not.

Somewhere in this milieu of tasks, the central work of the teacher is often overlooked—that of engaging students in learning. Although educational reform ideas are abundant, reforms will not make a difference unless classroom teachers have the time and resources to prepare lessons and teach students. Teachers must be allowed to focus on teaching and learning. They need uninterrupted class time to teach and time during the day to collaborate with colleagues, plan lessons, and assess student learning. They need respite from the paperwork and other nonteaching activities that consume their time. As experts in teaching and academic areas, they need input into decisions that affect their teaching and the learning of their students.

Successful principals know that the quality of education in their school depends on teachers having time to teach. They take steps to rid teachers of as many extraneous duties as possible by hiring paraprofessionals, securing volunteers, whatever it takes to give teachers time to prepare lessons and teach students. They regard teaching time as sacred—no announcements, interruptions, or capricious schedule changes. They prowl the hallways and classrooms so they understand teachers' needs and issues. They regard teachers as experts in teaching and seek their advice in decisions that affect them. They are creative in arranging school time for teachers to collaborate and plan. When teachers struggle, they support and help them. They tailor professional growth to meet each teacher's developmental needs. They acknowledge and celebrate individual teacher efforts and success with recognition and praise; they say thank you for a job well done.

In an era fraught with criticism of teachers and schools, teachers need to hear appreciation for their efforts. For many teachers, their positive reinforcement is derived from seeing their students learn and the occasional parent who sends a positive note. Although the majority of parents may be pleased, the ones heard from are those who are not. Almost daily, parents hear disheartening media accounts of the dismal state of education and the poor quality of teachers. Principals can make a difference by becoming the lead cheerleader and coach for teachers: celebrating their successes, encouraging them during challenges, and helping those who need assistance.

WHAT THE RESEARCH SAYS

The notion that the work of a teacher is difficult and demanding is not a new concept. In a 1983 essay, Shulman observed, "Teaching is impossible.

If we simply add together all that is expected of a typical teacher and take note of the circumstances in which those activities are to be carried out, the sum makes greater demands than any individual can possibly fulfill" (1983/2004, p. 51). Not only does the problem remain unresolved, in recent decades the role and workload of teachers has expanded. The 2003–2004 Schools and Staffing Survey reported that public school teachers were contracted to work 37.7 hours per week, but in reality performed school-related work an average of 52.8 hours per week (Strizek, Pittsonberger, Riordan, Lyter, & Orlofsky, 2006). Heightened social expectations, demands for accountability, and state and federal legislation, such as the No Child Left Behind Act (2001), have intensified the role and daily work of classroom teachers (Hargreaves, 1994). The workload of teachers even captured the attention of *New York Times* columnist, Samuel Freedman (2007), who dedicated a column to the plight of one teacher of English language learners who reported being so overwhelmed with the avalanche of paperwork and standardized testing that the first six weeks of school had elapsed before she had time to teach.

Exacerbating the stress, is the fact that students' performance is influenced by factors that lie outside teachers' control (Huberman, 2005). Teachers are responsible for educating students from all socioeconomic, cultural, religious, and geographic areas of society (Eltis & Crump, 2003). Those who critique teachers' performance seldom take this vast demographic diversity into consideration.

Although the workload has increased, fewer resources are available. Teachers are asked to do more in the same amount of time with fewer resources, a situation that fosters chronic overload (Eltis & Crump, 2003; Vandenberghe & Huberman, 1999). The website of the New South Wales Teachers Federation notes that authorities exploit the commitment and professionalism of teachers by expecting them to accept broadened roles and workloads without extending appropriate resources, including release time for reflection and planning.

Teachers would be more effective if given the necessary time to teach, plan, and collaborate with one another. Improvement of these three factors is likely to improve student achievement, improve teacher satisfaction, and lead to higher teacher retention. A study by Moore (2009) revealed that teachers believed in the benefits of collaboration and were in support of participation. Their main concern was when to conduct teacher collaboration without taking time away from students. Ironically, although the literature touts the importance of teacher collaboration and planning, many teachers do not have time for either activity. Planning occurs at the close of an exhausting workday and collaboration consists of conversations in the hallway between classes or in the lunchroom—unless the teacher has supervision duties (North Carolina Association of Educators, 2001).

Teachers teach because they want to make a difference in the lives of students. They want to feel part of a worthwhile endeavor (Glickman et al., 2010) and make a difference in the world (Kouzes & Posner, 2002). Without a principal to provide a supportive working environment and affirmation, however, the effect of their contributions can be clouded by the daily grind. According to one of the principals interviewed, "Teachers want to work with someone supportive and are more willing to follow principals who offer support." Principals can let teachers know that their role is important and they make a difference by ensuring that each teacher

- Feels known and valued as a person.
- Feels part of a worthwhile endeavor.
- Feels safe in the school environment.
- Feels part of a team effort.
- Feels appreciated for efforts.
- Feels recognized for accomplishments.
- Feels ideas and contributions are valued.
- Feels informed about what is going on in the school.
- Feels included in decisions and changes that affect them.
- Feels safe to try new ideas and seek assistance. (Brock & Grady, 2009, p. 99)

WHAT WORKS IN PRACTICE

Principals reported practices they used to support teachers, honor their expertise, and ensure they had time and resources to perform their job:

> When teachers have difficulties with students or problems with parents, be supportive. Get involved; help them out. If there was a problem with the teacher's actions, discuss it in private.

> I had a parent out to kill me because he wanted to get his child into a certain high school, and due to a report on his records, was fearful the child would not be accepted. He wanted the information expunged; the teacher was under a lot of pressure. When he came to me I told him I would not change it. I rechecked the information; the teacher was correct, and the report would not be changed. The teacher knew that I would back her decision. You have to build up that kind of trust.

Although the principal needs to be hands on … it is also important to give teachers a certain amount of autonomy. Trying to micromanage a school is counterproductive; staff [members] feel they are not valued and cannot make decisions for their students. There needs to be a balance between unilateral decisions and community decisions.

If a goal is important and staff [members] are asked to participate, give them extra time to perform the task or something by way of compensation.

If you say something is important, then put resources to it. If you give a person a job, give them extra time or something [in the form of compensation] for it. I have no respect for delegation dumping. If you put resources to the job, the message conveyed is that it is important.

One principal's solution for providing collaboration time:

When teachers complained that they did not have enough time to plan together, my assistant and I decided to go into the classrooms every Monday afternoon. We hired another teacher to help out a half day. [Now, the three] teachers in each grade level have time to sit down together during school hours and work out exactly what they plan to teach while we work with their students. As an added benefit, spending time in classrooms put us (principal and assistant principal) in touch with the level of student learning that is occurring and [makes us] more aware of the problems teachers experience.

TAKE ACTION

Ask the teachers to rate the following personal statements:

Use the scale from 1 (lowest) to 5 (highest) and check the box of your response:					
In the school:	*1*	*2*	*3*	*4*	*5*
My role as teacher is honored and respected.					
I am known and valued as a person.					
I am part of a worthwhile endeavor.					
I am part of a team effort.					
I am recognized for my accomplishments.					
I feel my ideas and contributions are valued.					
I am informed about what is going on in the school.					
I am included in decisions and changes that affect me.					
I feel physically safe in the school environment.					
I am encouraged to try new ideas.					
I am encouraged when I struggle.					
I feel comfortable asking for assistance.					
I am given adequate time to collaborate with colleagues.					
I have adequate material resources to teach.					
I am supported in disagreements with parents.					
I receive useful professional development.					
I receive constructive feedback on my teaching.					

Average the scores for each item. Note those that are in the upper 50% and take action to continue these items. Identify items that are in the lower 50%. Create an action plan for improvement.

An Action Plan	
Items That Need Improvement	*Steps to Take*

Tip 12

Do the Right Thing—Be Accountable for Decisions

[The leaders we admire] didn't get up in the morning and say, "I think I am going to change the world." ... They were groundbreakers who believed in themselves and the fact that right was right and wrong was wrong.

—Boesch, 2009, p. 169

Successful principals strive to do the right thing every day and in all situations. They became leaders out of a desire to serve the needs of others. They possess internal accountability. When faced with difficult decisions, they are guided by ethics, the right thing to do.

Although elements of several prominent theories were obvious in their behaviors, the successful principals we met are best described as servant leaders. Servant leadership is a philosophy and practice of leadership, first coined by Robert Greenleaf. Servant leaders achieve success for their organizations by prioritizing attention to the needs of their colleagues and the individuals they serve. They view themselves as stewards of their organization's human, financial, and physical resources.

According to Greenleaf, "The great leader is seen as a servant first ... [The person they are] down deep inside" is not something "bestowed, assumed, and not to be taken away" (1991, p. 2). They do what it is right because it is the right thing to do. A prime example was Mr. Peterson, a high school principal who, although the school met the legal standards of the Americans With Disabilities Act, petitioned the school board for more extensive accommodations because he believed it was "the right thing to do. If we truly want to serve all of the people who use this school, we need to move beyond the narrow confines of the law and make the building accessible for everyone."

Servant leaders want to serve rather than lead. "The person who is servant first, is more likely to persevere and refine his hypothesis on what serves another's highest priority needs than is the person who is leader first and who later serves out of prompting of conscience or in conformity with normative expectations" (Greenleaf, 1991, p. 8). People respond to these leaders because they are proven and trusted.

Servant leaders try new ideas, offer solutions, and are willing to accept the risk of failure and the promise of success. They are solutions oriented, not confined by established norms. They are cognizant that change takes time and tenacious in pursuing their goals. Clearly, it is less demanding to choose safer alternatives or take the stance that the problem is too great or entrenched for one person to handle. Consequently, some leaders avoid or retreat from involvement in an uncomfortable or difficult situation. Other leaders play the blame game, becoming so absorbed in dissecting what is wrong that they fail to act. Others become impatient because reform is slow and choose to destroy the system, on the assumption that a new beginning will fix everything. Servant leaders are more like Sisyphus (2010), who accepted his rock and found satisfaction in dealing with it. They are a spark of hope in the world, "solitary individuals whose deeds and works every day negate frontiers and the crudest implications of history" (Greenleaf, 1991, p. 5).

Treatment of others is grounded in an abiding respect for the dignity and value of all people. No one is invisible or insignificant. Servant leaders choose to lead because they seek the highest priorities of others. They treat everyone, regardless of position, title, wealth, or education, with respect—not only at work but in all facets of their lives. They are humble and self-assured individuals who make others feel valued, but also care enough to challenge others to grow. Their actions inspire people to follow them.

Servant leaders take responsibility for their errors. When they make a mistake, they admit it rather than making excuses or shifting blame to others. They are known to admit, "I thought the initiative would work, but I was wrong." They apologize when their actions hurt others. They are sincere and make amends. People are usually willing to forgive, even admire, a leader who admits an error and corrects it. People are equally quick to condemn a leader who makes excuses, blames others, or tries to conceal mistakes. Media reports about the misdeeds, excuses, and apologies of public figures are replete with examples.

A professor recalled the admiration he had for a university official who sought him out and apologized for his rude behavior during a meeting, admitting, "I am sorry and embarrassed. I acted like an ass." A teacher recalled the admiration she maintained for a teacher from her high school days, who had apologized to her for losing his temper and unjustly lashing out at her. These poignant moments delivered lasting and powerful messages about the humility necessary for successful leadership.

WHAT THE RESEARCH SAYS

Successful leadership likely occurs at the intersection of many of the prominent theories that guide school leaders. Each theory has distinctive advantages and drawbacks. Some leaders are consciously guided by or strive within one motivating theory. Given the complexity of school leadership, however, principals likely call into play some aspect of all of the theories over time. We examine a few of the more prominent leadership theories: transformational and transactional leadership, total quality management, servant leadership, situational leadership, and instructional leadership.

The work of James Burns (1978) gave rise to the theories of transformational and transactional leadership. Burns defined transactional as trading one thing for another, whereas transformational referred to true change. Using Burns's model as a platform, Bass (1985), Bass and Avolio (1994), and Leithwood (1994) developed the transformational leadership model for education. Essential leadership components include personal attention to individual members, involving staff in innovative problem solving, communicating high expectations, and modeling appropriate character and behavior.

Total quality management (TQM) was founded by Edward Deming (1986) for the world of business. The model was used to provide a framework for post–World War II Japan to restore its manufacturing base and for U.S. firms to improve the quality of their products and services. The model evolved to include five factors that influenced educational leadership: change agency, teamwork, continuous improvement, trust building, and replacement of short-term goals with goals more focused on long-term growth.

Servant leadership arose from the writings of Robert Greenleaf (1970, 1977), who believed that the basis for effective leadership was a desire to help others. Rather than being at the top of the organizational hierarchy, the leader occupies a position in the center. Interaction with all strata of the organization is central to the leader's understanding of personal needs, ability to heal conflicts, stewardship of resources, development of staff leadership skills, and effective listening.

Situational leadership is ascribed to the work of Paul Hersey and Kenneth Blanchard (Blanchard, Carew, Parisi-Carew, 1991; Blanchard & Hersey, 1996;

Blanchard, Zigarmi, & Zigarmi, 1985; Hersey, Blanchard, & Johnson, 2001). The premise of situational leadership is the leader's adaptation to the followers' ability to perform specific tasks. Leadership styles match maturity level and willingness to perform tasks under four conditions: (1) when followers are unwilling or unable, the leader directs the actions with little concern for relationships (telling); (2) when followers are unable but willing, the leader provides direction and guidance in a more participative style (participating); (3) when followers are unwilling, the leaders persuades followers to engage in the task (selling); (4) when followers are willing and able, the leader trusts the individual to accomplish the task without interference (delegating).

Instructional leadership, although popular and mentioned frequently in the literature, is the least defined. Among its proponents are Wilma Smith and Richard Andrews (1989), who identify four roles of an instructional leader: resource provider, instructional resource, communicator, and visible presence. The reflection-growth (RG) model of Blasé and Blasé (1999) suggests that leaders should facilitate the following behaviors: the study of teaching and learning, collaborative efforts among teachers, coaching relationships among teachers, using instructional research to make decisions, and using the principles of adult learning for professional development. Glickman et al. (2010) suggest direct assistance to teachers, development of collaborative groups, provision of effective staff and curriculum development, and use of action research to improve instruction.

WHAT WORKS IN PRACTICE

Principals shared their views on accountability:

> When I took the position, I was told there were several issues to address so I came in thinking I would fix *everything*. I didn't consider why the previous principal had not fixed these problems or how the staff felt about the school or any of the issues. I barged ahead and in my attempt to fix things I totally antagonized a large proportion of the staff. When I returned after being away from school for a few days, I discovered a note written on a classroom wallboard that said, "Is there anyone in this school who likes Mrs. T.?" I shared my hurt feelings with a friend, who said, 'Have you ever thought of saying "sorry?" You have offended people and need to begin again. So I said "sorry," and asked, "What would you like me to do?" I discovered that there are two things people like to hear. One is "sorry" when you have erred; and the other is, "What would you like me to do?" They might not have a solution, but they know they don't like what you're doing. And they like to be asked.

If you and your teachers don't make mistakes it means you aren't taking any risks; you are just doing the same old things. I tell teachers that it is OK to make mistakes, but I expect them to admit them and learn from them. When I make a mistake, I tell them so. We discuss our errors in private; in public I support them and expect the same.

[I tell teachers that] what you see is what you get. You will know where you stand. I will offer you loyalty and honesty, but also ask that you return it. If there is an issue, we will work together to solve it. I will assume that I can trust you and I will be extremely disappointed if I discover otherwise. Come and tell me if you have done something that will result in [a parent] calling to tell me her side of [a situation]. If there is an issue we will work together to solve it.

TAKE ACTION

1. Identify your leadership strengths. What are your plans to capitalize on these behaviors?

2. Identify your leadership shortcomings. What improvements will you make?

Questions for Reflection

- Would your staff members say that you stand up for what is right even when it is unpopular?
- Do you make decisions based on what is right, rather than on what is easy, expedient, or expected?
- Do you acknowledge your errors, admit mistakes, and learn from them?
- Did a person in authority ever apologize to you? How did your feelings toward that person change? How could this behavior be useful for you?
- Does your behavior toward someone change because of "who" they are: their occupation, title, degree, age? Consider how you welcome and respond to everyone with whom you interact in your personal and professional life: teachers, parents, students, staff members, and those who serve you in stores and restaurants?
- How do you make people around you feel valued (teachers, parents, students, staff members, family members, and friends)?

(Continued)

(Continued)

- How do you challenge and help colleagues and staff members grow? Do you mentor others?
- Do people with whom you interact feel better or somehow improved by knowing you?
- Which leadership theory best describes your leadership behavior?

Part III

School Community

School leadership is not a solo operation; it is all about people working together. Leading a school requires skill in facilitating cooperation and productive behaviors from all members of the school community. To understand successful leadership, we explored the practices of successful leaders within the context of their school environment—the school community.

Tip 13

Create Trusting Relationships

- Know the population and community.
- Care about people; make them feel valued.
- Share your expectations.
- Listen to everyone's opinions.
- Treat everyone fairly.
- Keep your promises.

Successful schools are composed of teams of people working in concert toward a common goal—a task that requires trust in the leader and relational trust between members. We listen to and are influenced by people we trust. Trusting relationships, however, are not achieved by virtue of title. Trusting relationships must be earned, nurtured, and maintained.

The first step in earning trust is getting to know the people and letting them get to know you. Staff members, students, teachers, and parents are rightfully anxious when a new principal is appointed. They analyze every word and action to determine the leader's trustworthiness. After all, the leadership of the new principal will have a critical impact on the professional lives of employees, the well-being of students, and a long-term effect on the direction and success of the school.

- Earn trust by sharing your philosophy of teaching, learning, discipline, and interest in parental involvement.
- Assure parents that you will uphold high academic expectations, yet demonstrate care and concern for their children.
- Assure teachers that you will work in concert with them.

- Listen and learn before making decisions and promises.
- When you do make a promise—keep it.
- When you make a mistake—admit it.
- Keep confidences.
- Make everyone feel valued.
- Show that you are interested, caring, and approachable—someone who will support and work with others.
- Meet with as many people as possible and listen to their views and opinions. Get to know staff members as people as well as professionals. How well you listen and the interest you show in people and their opinions will be key factors in developing and maintaining the trust of the staff and community.

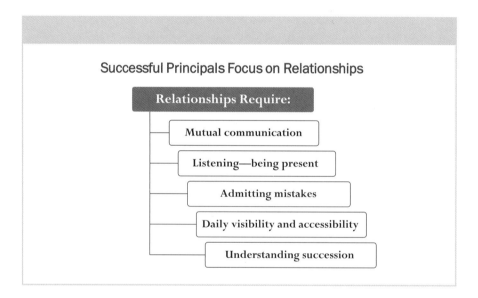

Successful Principals Focus on Relationships

Relationships Require:

- Mutual communication
- Listening—being present
- Admitting mistakes
- Daily visibility and accessibility
- Understanding succession

WHAT THE RESEARCH SAYS

Research studies support the importance of trust in successful leaders (Kouzes & Posner, 2002). Teachers need to know that the principal cares about student learning, is interested in helping them improve instruction, and has the expertise to do so (Henson, 2010).

Relational trust is developed through the many exchanges that occur between members of the school community. Relational trust requires respect for each person's role in the school, competence in their execution of respective roles, personal regard for others, and personal integrity—maintaining consistency between words and actions (Bryk & Schneider, 2002). In a study of the effect of relational trust on student learning and governance, Bryk and Schneider discovered a positive relationship between student learning and effective school governance and high levels of relational trust.

Trust is not freely given. Instead, it must be earned and modeled through honesty and ethical practices (Barth, 2006; Irons & Aller, 2007). Trust within organizations originates from four areas: (1) a climate that is conducive to trust; (2) the character of the leader; (3) standards of conduct that are mandated, modeled, enforced, and rewarded; and (4) purposeful cultivation of a culture of trust (Armour, 2007). According to Bryk and Schneider (2002), "Trust within a school faculty is grounded in common understandings about what students should learn, how instruction should be conducted, and how teachers and students should behave with one another" (p. 130).

To create trusting relationships, there must be a culture of open feedback. Students and teachers need to be empowered to share their opinions without fear of reprisal and feel assured of support when they attempt new approaches.

To initiate and maintain trusting relationships, a system of mutual communication must be in place. "Trust is built and experienced within the context of multifaceted communication systems … [that are] open and fluid, include feedback loops, and [are] practiced by everyone in the school" (Lambert, 1998, pp. 79–80).

Watzlawick, Beavin Bavelas, and Jackson (1967) identified five axioms that explain the complex system of human communication and offer a guide to the formation of relational symmetry in communications that can lead to trusting relationships.

1. The first axiom reminds us that humans are always communicating. We cannot not communicate. Actions and inactions convey messages, although they may be unintended.

2. The second axiom reminds us that all interactions contain both an explicit message and information on how the message is to be understood. The metacommunication offers information about the relationship aspect.

3. The third axiom addresses the way that interactants group or punctuate their communications into smaller units.

4. The fourth axiom acknowledges the digital and analogic forms of human communication. Digital communication is composed of words while analog communication is composed of nonverbal forms. Digital communication corresponds primarily to content, whereas analogic communication expresses the relationship between interactors.

5. The fifth axiom denotes the symmetrical or complementary nature of the communications and is based on the equality or difference among interactors. Symmetrical relationships are based on equality, whereas complementary relationships are unequal.

WHAT WORKS IN PRACTICE

All of the principals interviewed emphasized the importance of developing positive relationships. One principal explained, "I think developing relationships with everyone is important, no matter whether it's the maintenance person, technology guy, the pastor, parents." For the principals, their goal was establishing mutual trust and respect. Critical to relationship building was visibility and accessibility in the building and on the grounds.

Factors That Can Affect Acceptance. A few principals mentioned succession issues that affected their initial acceptance. Stability of the school, leadership turnover, the new principal's reputation, and loyalty to a previous administration were factors that affected their initial acceptance into the community. Principals who entered stable schools with little turnover and principals who were well-known to the school community experienced greater acceptance. One principal explained, "The fact that I was well-known in the community was a factor in my acceptance. Although people did not know what kind of a principal I would be, they knew me and probably had a good idea."

By contrast, principals who entered schools that had experienced instability, rapid leadership turnover, or had lost a beloved leader struggled to gain acceptance. One principal described his struggle: "I came into a chaotic situation in which there had been a lot of turnover. Although I had a lot of experience, people were skeptical about me; teachers had the perception that I would be a short-timer so they didn't take me seriously." A high school principal who replaced a beloved leader said, "The comparative issues and loyalty factor with the previous administration were difficult to overcome; I struggled to get people on board. A lot of teachers left at the end of the year, which was challenging. However, hiring new people who were loyal to me improved the situation."

A middle school principal who succeeded a leader who had died said, "I don't think there is anything more difficult than replacing someone who dies. No matter what that person did or didn't do, people can't move past the loss. All the good things the person did are remembered and things not so good are forgotten."

Strategies to Win Acceptance. Principals acknowledged the importance of communication in developing trusting relationships with the school community. They used meetings with individuals, small groups of teachers, and large group presentations as tools in establishing trust. Principals emphasized the importance of admitting mistakes as critical to nurturing trust and respect. They identified listening as a critical skill. Do not be afraid of being silent. In the words of one principal, "Listen, listen, then listen some more." A high school principal suggested, "Stop, focus on teachers [who want to talk], and give them 100% attention. Ask people how their lives are going; ask about their kids and grandkids. This is an opportunity to build relationships."

Although they acknowledged the importance of relationships with staff, principals cautioned against becoming overly involved in teachers' personal lives. An elementary principal explained, "I am there for teachers during the tragedies in their lives—when the divorce is imminent or he has gambled away the mortgage … but they know that we both have jobs to do. I will cry with them, I will hug them, and we will get through the rough spots in life together, but personal problems cannot erode the everyday environment of the school. I need a teacher who can put aside personal issues, stand up in front of the class, and do the job. If that cannot happen, I send people home and hire a sub."

Principals' suggestions for building relationships with staff focused on listening.

> People want to know that you will listen to them; that you do not believe you have all the answers. When you first arrive at a school, [staff members and parents] want to know that you are willing to learn what all the issues are: what to touch and what not to touch. They want a principal who listens!

> A successful principal is a good communicator (listening being the key part). As I began the year, one of the first things I did was meet with each of my staff members (certified and classified) and spoke with them about what they liked most about the building/atmosphere, liked least, wanted to change, and about themselves. Each staff member shared with me that they felt this was a great way to start the year. It made them feel like they were part of the decision-making atmosphere of the building.

> The worst thing you can do is go in with a set change in mind—coming in with what you think is right. That's very unwise because that may not match with what you see. Instead, you need to go in and listen, listen, and listen some more. And ask questions—not to make people defensive, but rather to gain understanding. Encourage a lot of people to give you input. When I did this, I found that I had a much better idea of things that needed to happen. Also, the more I listened, the more readily people were willing to make changes.

Having the patience to deal with the diverse personalities in the building is important—along with being flexible to make changes and adapt to the changes of each person.

Make personal connections to establish relationships. It makes people feel good to know you care about them.

Teachers Have Their Own Ideas to Share. Teachers were quick to point out the importance of being genuine. One teacher offered the example of a principal who distributed birthday cards but did not greet the teacher in the hall.

The principal I worked for always put a birthday card in my mailbox; although the personal touch was nice, this same person would walk by me in the hall and not say a word. I never understood that.

By contrast, another teacher mentioned,

During the first month of school, my principal made it a point to get to know all of the staff both professionally and personally. On the second or third visit with her, she made a point to ask how my daughter and son were doing—by name. This showed me that she was truly interested in me and my family.

The following are teachers' suggestions for principals:

Establishing relationships with staff is key to being an effective leader. The principal must take time to get to know all staff. When an administrator takes the time to know people, they feel valued—which is the first step in creating trust. Once relationships are established, it allows for more open and honest discussion—people can disagree and discuss issues when there is trust.

[Successful principals] welcome individuals into the school: students, staff, parents, community members. When people are made to feel welcome by the leader of the school, they feel part of a team and will want to do their best because they feel the leader is doing his/her best for them.

Know your staff members as people, what motivates them, information about their families.

Principals new to a building should start building relationships by meeting with ALL staff individually. The principal needs to know if there are recurring themes for both great things about the school and negative things about the school.

Ask teachers what changes they would make and why? Even if those things won't necessarily change, it lets teachers know that the principal cares about their feelings. Ask for teachers' ideas and opinions on school topics.

Principals must believe they are the teacher of teachers and want to be personally involved with the staff. Talk with teachers about their educational philosophy; challenge their ideas; help them become better teachers.

Be aware of the nuances of teachers' behavior. Notice changes in people's usual behavior, when something seems different; reach out to teachers when you sense something is wrong.

Let teachers know you care about their personal and professional well-being by having an open-door policy where teachers feel welcome to come to your office and discuss any issues.

Have a pleasant, approachable demeanor: Nothing says "Don't bother communicating" better than a closed door, snapped responses, and a grumpy demeanor.

Respect the differences in staff. Do not show favoritism or give preferential treatment to staff whose educational philosophy more closely matches yours.

Visit classrooms for brief observations; doing so lets teachers know that you care about them and their class.

Create Relationships With Students. Spending time with students was important to the principals we interviewed. A middle school principal said, "It's the relationship you form with the kids that is key to how they behave in school. Once they know you, they don't want to disappoint you." Principals agreed that student discipline problems tend to diminish when the principal has a positive relationship with students and treats them fairly. All of the principals mentioned the importance of interacting with students. The format they used varied according to type and size of the school and the age of the students. Principals viewed relationships with students as closely connected to their work as instructional leaders.

Create Relationships With Parents. Principals wanted parents to feel welcome to bring suggestions or concerns to them. Two principals reported spending time outside in the morning and at dismissal, greeting students and waiting with them for their rides to arrive. An elementary principal explained, "You can gain a lot of trust in those 15 to 20 minutes by letting students and parents see you are a person. One day while I was standing there, wearing eight layers and freezing, a mom drove up and handed me a cup of hot coffee. Parents care."

Additionally, principals practiced and encouraged teachers to engage in frequent, personal communications with parents. A high school principal explained, "It's the human contact piece of parent–teacher communications that is very important. Pick up the phone and call them. But do not wait until there is a problem to have that first conversation." A middle school principal said she encouraged direct rather than electronic communication for herself and her teachers, saying,

My rule is after one e-mail, you pick up the phone. If you are talking on the phone, you can hear the emotion, frustration, and despair … instead of getting e-mail in capital letters. Also, use restraint—reread and think a few minutes—before hitting the "send button."

Create Relationships With Community Members. A middle school principal whose community consisted of a large population of elderly people offered an excellent example of how to involve the senior citizens in the school. She explained, "It is important to me that people who were part of our past and continue to support us today are included in our school. The students need to know that these are the people who came before them, who are still supportive of them today, and toward whom they have a responsibility." She initiated service projects for the students to provide assistance to senior citizens in the neighborhood, has senior citizen luncheons in the school cafeteria, and sponsors a reminiscence project in which teenagers interview and write the life stories of the senior citizens. They hold a school celebration when students present the spiral-bound biographies to their senior citizen partners.

Principals in Catholic Schools Need Trusting Relationships With Pastors. Principals in Catholic elementary schools agreed that the relationship between the principal of the school and the pastor of the parish was a major factor in their success and job satisfaction. The uniqueness of the leadership roles makes it critical for principals and pastors to (1) clarify individual roles and responsibilities, (2) establish a trusting relationship, and (3) meet regularly to discuss school issues (Brock & Fraser, 2001). Principals who had a positive working relationship with their pastors said it contributed to their job success and satisfaction. Principals who had experienced frequent turnover of pastors reported it was detrimental to the establishment of trust and led to adversarial and unsatisfying working relationships.

Two of the principals attributed their success, in part, to the excellent working relationships they had with their pastors. One principal explained, "I have worked with two pastors. Even though each of them had their own leadership style, they allowed me to do my job, didn't micromanage me. Yet, if I needed assistance, input, or grounding, I could go to them."

Other principals reported that strained relationships made success much more difficult. One principal said, "I have had several different pastors, all of whom had different gifts and talents. I could communicate with and depend on some of the pastors; with others the relationship was adversarial. That causes a lot of stress as you try to be successful in spite of the strained relationship." Another principal concurred, "We had a turnover of three pastors in three years—each of whom wanted to leave their mark. The pressure on everybody wanting to do it their own way … was a bit of a challenge."

TAKE ACTION

1. Meet with everyone in the school community.

    If you are new to a school, consider how you want to approach the initial meetings. Will you meet with each teacher, meet with small groups of teachers, or will the first encounter be a presentation to the entire faculty? How will you get acquainted with parents?

2. Share your beliefs and opinions.

Say just enough to enable the listener to understand your meaning; often communication is nullified by saying too much (Greenleaf, 1991). Share your style of leadership and communication, how you perceive your role, your vision for the school, and how you plan to interact with, supervise, and evaluate staff. Share your definition of good teaching, an orderly classroom, professional behavior, and appropriate dress.

Before speaking to a group of staff members or parents, write out the message you plan to share. Since each group is interested in different aspects of your background and leadership, the information you share will be different. Teachers want to know your educational beliefs, expectations, leadership style, and how you will treat them. Parents want to know your standards, how you will interact with them, and how you will treat their children. Before you deliver the message in public, read it to a friend or family member and obtain their feedback on clarity and tone. Tape-record your message. Since this is the first impression you project, be sure the information and tone of the message convey the image you desire. Remember, first impressions are lasting. An undesirable first impression can be difficult to overcome.

3. Listen more than you speak.

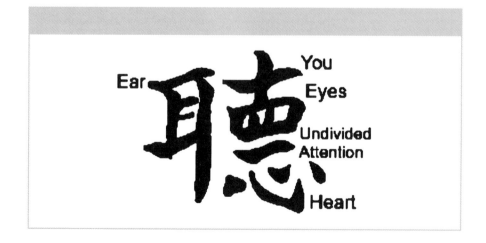

The Chinese characters that make up the verb "to listen" tell us something significant about the skill. To be a good listener, you must listen with ears, eyes, and heart, giving undivided attention to the speaker. Listen carefully and with undivided attention. Before you speak, reflect on Greenleaf's (1991) admonition, "In saying what I have in mind will I really improve on the silence?" (p. 11).

- What is your plan for learning the opinions and views of the staff?
- How will you identify the opinions and wishes of parents?

4. Consider the opinions of everyone. Create a system of mutual communication and a climate in which people feel free to make suggestions, discuss opposing ideas, and make mistakes. Be careful not to show favoritism to any person or group or to be seduced by "squeaky wheels." Showing favoritism triggers resentment and distrust.

5. Remember that staff members have personal lives. Be thoughtful in scheduling. Be understanding of family issues. Make staff wellness a priority.

6. Keep your promises. Gather all the facts before making a promise; then follow through. Nothing destroys credibility and trust more quickly than breaking a promise or asking for opinions and then ignoring them.

7. Evaluate and improve the quality of your relationships with staff members. List all of the people who work in your school—certified and noncertified. Identify individuals who are neglected and areas that are ignored. Use the information to create an action plan to strengthen relationships.

Create an action plan to strengthen relationships.

Name	Action Plan	Priority	Target Date

Questions for Reflection

- Have you ever worked with a school leader who you did not trust? What could that person have done to win your trust?
- Reflect on a principal who had the trust of a school community. What did the principal do to earn and maintain that trust?
- What actions do you need to take to improve the trust level within your school?
- Have you ever worked for someone who did not value you as a person? How did you want to be treated?
- Have you ever worked with a leader who did not value your opinions, one who showed favoritism? How did you feel? What did you want from the leader?
- Do you value the people in your school? Do you value their opinions? How do they know that?

Tip 14

Context Matters: Adjust Your Leadership to the School's Population

Stand up for your kids.

—Secondary principal

- Know the problems of students.
- Understand the problems parents encounter.
- Be aware of economic and social circumstances of the community.
- Know the history and current organizational needs of the school.
- Adjust your leadership to the function and mission of the school.

Context matters. Strategies that yield success in one school context might invite failure in another. Successful principals use similar practices and strategies; however, they adjust those practices and strategies to fit the contextual needs of a specific school population. A comprehensive understanding of the needs of a school population and the expectations of the community are central to determining appropriate leadership strategies and a direction for action. Principals report having to change their leadership approaches to meet the needs of different cultures, geographic areas, socioeconomic levels, and school sizes.

Leaders who move between public and faith-based schools must adapt to differing expectations in the areas of vision, mission, leadership as well as different operational and governance systems. Religion-based schools approach the task of educating children with a different perspective from that of public education. Schools with a religious affiliation rely on religious principles and values to provide the basis for the school's vision and mission. The education of youth is viewed as an integral part of the mission of the church (Mulligan, 1999).

School leaders in faith-based schools are expected to be spiritual as well as instructional leaders (Belmonte & Cranston, 2009). Each of these issues is critical to the success of individuals who strive to be successful in schools with religious affiliations.

Successful leaders begin each year and each new position by examining the needs and expectations of the school population, the parents, and the larger community. Each experience and every school year brings changing circumstances that demand leadership adaptations, adjustments, and sometimes, additional training. For example, principals new to Catholic schools may find benefit from courses and workshops related to leadership in a faith-based school environment. Ideally, those who aspire to Catholic school leadership receive preparation in spiritual and theological formation in addition to training in academic and managerial aspects of administration (Smith & Nuzzi, 2007). However, not all preparation programs equip principals for the unique challenges of Catholic education; thus, it is the responsibility of the principal to acquire spiritual and theological formation. Although the adoption of new skills may stretch one's comfort level, the final outcome will be more success.

WHAT THE RESEARCH SAYS

Every school is unique in context, and successful principals respond to that context. Their decisions and actions are responsive to social, cultural, political, and economic factors embedded in the school population and larger community.

In a review of literature on successful principals, Leithwood et al. (2008) contend that successful leaders draw on the same repertoire of administrative strategies. However, their actions and decisions are influenced by interaction with others in relationship to the performance of specific tasks. Similar conclusions are reported by Spillane, Halverson, and Diamond, who maintain that leadership emerges through "interaction with other people and the environment" (2004, p. 8).

Leithwood, Louis, Anderson, and Wahlstrom (2004) suggest that there are differences in administrative competencies needed to lead different kinds of schools, particularly in terms of organizational context, size, and geographical location. They offer examples, such as successful principals reporting that more direct and top-down forms of leadership are more effective in inner-city schools than in suburban settings. Successful principals in elementary schools require a more extensive curricular knowledge than secondary principals, who rely on department heads for such knowledge. Principals of smaller schools can influence and model instruction through direct engagement with teachers, whereas principals in larger schools need to rely on indirect means of influencing instruction. Leadership initiatives must be context specific.

Leithwood et al. (2004) additionally suggest that selection processes for principals should match the abilities and situational knowledge of the candidate with specific requirements for the school context in which they will be working. Davis, Darling-Hammond, LaPointe, and Meyerson (2005) note that context is central to success in performing the important functions of instruction, community building, change management, and addressing the needs of particular school populations. They identify factors that require consideration including school type, demographics, culture, and economic stability. According to Davis et al. (2005), the notions of generic leadership are being replaced by more contextual notions of leadership. Context is an important factor in areas of instruction, community building, and change management and in schools that serve students with specific backgrounds or needs.

WHAT WORKS IN PRACTICE

The principals we spoke with emphasized the importance of understanding and responding to the contextual circumstances of a school. Their success depended on their ability to address variations in circumstances, such as ethnicity and primary language of the population, size of the school, poverty in the wider community, income level of parents, students' level of physical aggression, students' academic level, prevalence of child abuse, and level of parental involvement. Principals explained how they needed to adapt to their school settings:

The person you are at one school is not necessarily the person you will become at another. I would like to believe that you are chosen for or select a specific school because of what you will bring.

What is successful in one socioeconomic area may not be a successful strategy in another. I am very different in my second school than I was in my first school. The school is different … what worked in the previous, more multicultural school, does not work in this predominately Anglo-Saxon school. I have had to change in response to that need. You have to provide a certain kind of leadership to move a school forward, so I am different in the way I do some things.

It's important to know your clients and be able to be in touch and empathize with them. In my situation in the inner city, I had to do a lot of stretching to learn the family dynamics, the family dysfunctions, [and the situations that affect] the children that come into my building.

We are a school of great diversity and I was the white woman coming in. [Parents looked at me and thought,] who was I—dealing with children who were mostly African American? You have to know your people and they have to know you. Build their trust or it just won't work.

Although I attended and taught in nonpublic schools, when I was appointed principal of one, I realized I had no idea how to lead a non-public. My graduate preparation had not included the role and responsibilities required of a leader in a faith-based setting. It was on-the-job learning for me … the hard way.

One principal's response to an impoverished school population:

When Mrs. L. was appointed as the principal of a downtown, urban school, she knew her role needed to differ from what it had been in her previous role in a more suburban setting. The population was transient; several families often occupied the same dwelling; thus she needed to find out who would be attending the school and to welcome families who were reluctant. She and her staff took to the streets to meet the people. They talked with parents and students on street corners, visited local businesses, walked the routes children would be walking to school, and welcomed people to visit the school. She brought community resources to the school to help families.

One year she raised money, struck a deal with a local department store, and bought a coat for every student in the school. Since many of the students had never owned something new, she had the store bring in samples and students were invited to select the style they wanted and the size they needed.

She collaborated with a charity that received household donations to bring home furnishings to the school to distribute to anyone who needed them. The first year, seven hundred families received assistance.

TAKE ACTION

1. List the positive attributes of the school. What is working well in the school? What are its successes? What should not be touched or changed?

2. List the specific needs of the school: What needs to change to make students in the school successful?

3. Determine the current academic level of students. Where are they successful? In what areas is improvement needed? Work with teachers to identify realistic goals for improvement and an action plan to raise achievement. Raise expectations. Reward and applaud successes.

4. Determine the leadership strategies that will be most effective in this context. What do I need to do differently? What do I need to learn?

Questions for Reflection

What is the daily life of students? What problems do they bring to school? What problems do their parents face? What are their hopes for their children? What do they need and want from you and from the school? What do you need to do to help each student in the school succeed?

Get acquainted with the community and collect data. Become an expert on the history and culture of the school and wider community.

(Continued)

(Continued)

- Drive and walk around the neighborhood. What are the conditions of the buildings and streets?
- Review demographic data about the area. What are the problems and opportunities?
- Visit the businesses in the area; talk with the people who work in them. How do they view the school?
- Meet the parents. What do they think are the strengths and needs of the school?
- Talk with students. What do they like about their school? What needs to change?
- Meet the teachers. What do they think are the strengths and needs of the school?
- Read the local newspaper. What is reported on the school? What are the local problems?
- Identify differences in your background, gender, ethnicity, language, and socioeconomic level that might make the community reluctant to accept you. How are you different? How will you be viewed by parents and teachers? How can you earn their trust?
- Are you a new principal in a faith-based school? What assistance do you need in adapting to new role expectations? Where can you find that assistance?

Part IV

Teaching and Learning

S chools exist for the purpose of educating students. Every action that occurs in a school should be directed toward the ultimate goal of educating all students. Successful principals never lose sight of that goal and they are able to unite the school staff in a concerted effort to meet it.

Tip 15

Establish Learning as the Common Purpose

Principals who are successful create conditions that promote quality teaching and learning for *all* students. They are not larger-than-life leaders who think they can do it all. They get the job done by establishing a common purpose in their organizations. Everyone in the school, from teacher to custodian, knows their role and is willing to work toward the goal. The common purpose resonates throughout the building and noticeably drives decisions and behavior (Kurtzman, 2010).

Successful principals foster a sense of inclusiveness among personnel, ensuring that everyone understands their role (Kurtzman, 2010) in teaching, facilitating, or providing an environment that supports student learning. Although teachers are charged with delivering curriculum content, everyone in the school plays a role in enriching an environment that supports instruction and student well-being. Support personnel who provide nourishment, who keep the building functioning and clean, who make sure the office is running smoothly, and who care about students' well-being provide the foundational environment that enables teachers to teach and principals to lead. How many students have fond memories of a kind custodian, cafeteria worker, paraprofessional, or office assistant who took the time to listen, comfort, or encourage? Current and past students shared the importance of these individuals. A fifth-grade student said,

> My favorite person in the whole school retired; I will miss her so much.
> Her name is Mrs. Jones; she is a paraprofessional who comes into our
> classroom and helps us. She likes to talk with students and she is always
> so nice to us.

A message posted on a class reunion blog: "Do you guys remember the great cafeteria ladies, Mrs. Smith, Tucker, and Timmins and the good lunches they made for us? I posted a couple of photos of them. Does anyone remember the time Mrs. Timmins …?" Although we tend to think of teachers as having the primary contact, everyone who works in a school affects students, directly or indirectly. The combined attitudes and actions of all school personnel factor into the learning environment.

When teachers, support staff, and administrators operate from the singular purpose of improving student learning—seemingly unrelated, even unimportant daily tasks assume new meaning and importance. When everyone sees how their job contributes, it fosters positive attitudes and gives purpose to the daily grind. People feel good and work harder when they feel their jobs are important, they serve a purpose larger than themselves, and their contribution has value. It is the transformative power of people that enables the organization to continually improve itself. It takes a village to raise a child, and it takes an entire school to educate one.

WHAT THE RESEARCH SAYS

Kurtzman (2010) contends that the key to a highly successful organization is the creation of common purpose. Common purpose is achieved when personnel internalize the goals, purpose, and hopes of an institution. A sense of "we" develops, transforming the group into a dynamic, united force, willing to work tirelessly toward a singular goal. Although difficult to achieve, when common purpose occurs, the results are remarkable.

The role of the leader is to unite the people, establish the direction, and maintain group functioning. Rather than cheering from the sidelines, successful leaders must be connected with the group and have earned the right to lead by demonstrating that they understand the challenges and can do the job. Kurtzman (2010) cites examples of this practice in businesses, such as UPS, where most of the CEOs began their career driving a van or working in a warehouse, and Proctor & Gamble (founded in 1837), which has never brought in an outsider as CEO. A similar need exists in schools. Principals need to demonstrate that they know how to teach and understand the demands and challenges, and connect with personnel at all levels of the institution. They need to be willing to roll up their sleeves and get their hands dirty. As one elementary principal observed, "Good leaders never ask school personnel to do anything they are not willing to do themselves."

Leithwood et al. (2008) claim, "School leaders improve teaching and learning indirectly and most powerfully through their influence on staff motivation, commitment, and working conditions" (p. 27). Although much emphasis has been placed on the principal's contributions to building staff capacity, research suggests that overall, gains in that regard have been modest. Kurtzman (2010) concurs, noting that great leaders evoke emotion, such as pride and enthusiasm, in the people they lead, which are more powerful motivators than rewards and punishments.

Working conditions are, in part, a factor in the workplace culture. The nature of the culture influences how people perceive their role, respond to the demands, and attach meaning to their work (Schein, 1985). Culture, as defined by Hoy and Miskel (2008), is "a system of shared orientations that hold the unit together and give it distinctive identity" (p. 214). Bolman and Deal (1991) remind us that culture is both product and process, embodying the accumulated wisdom of the past while continually renewing itself as new members adopt old ways.

Culture is reflected symbolically, in stories, myths, ceremonies, and rituals that play a role in perpetuating a sense of orderliness and tradition, the way things are done. Although one might assume that norms adjust according to need—that is not the reality. Prevailing norms become entrenched and resistant to change, even when they are no longer useful and sometimes unhealthy.

Changing a school's culture requires concerted time and effort. Old norms must be examined and adjusted or replaced with more appropriate ones. Achieving a healthy school culture is an ongoing process that requires a team effort. Topchik (2001) suggests a four-step process for changing culture: (1) conduct an audit of existing norms, (2) describe the new norms, (3) develop an action plan for each norm change, and (4) implement the action plan that involves members of the school community.

WHAT WORKS IN PRACTICE

One principal shared her experience:

> I was frustrated with student untidiness and the custodian's daily complaints until a chance comment by a student provided the key to solving the problem. When I overheard a student dismiss the mess he left, saying, "Oh the custodian guy will clean it up," I realized that students viewed
>
> *(Continued)*

(Continued)

the custodian and his work as unimportant. He was a nameless, faceless person, and school cleanliness was not viewed as their problem. I needed to change attitudes. So I began the next school year by introducing the custodian to the students—one classroom at a time—told them his name, explained the importance of his job, and engaged students in a discussion of how they could help him keep our school clean. Students began to speak with the custodian in the hallway. He left notes of thanks when classrooms were left especially clean; students left apologies when they had an unavoidably messy project. Attitudes changed, mutual respect developed, and behaviors improved. School cleanliness improved. At the end of the year, the custodian told me that he enjoyed his work, and for the first time, felt like he was a part of the school team.

Observed in a school in Australia:

During an unannounced visit to a large school in Australia, one of the most memorable individuals was the school's maintenance engineer. He was on duty before anyone else arrived and when they did, the doors were unlocked, the lights were on, and homemade rolls waited in the staff's gathering room where he cheerfully greeted school staff as they arrived. The building and grounds were noticeably well maintained and attractive. When complimented about the appearance of the school, the principal gave full credit to the school's maintenance engineer, explaining that he was an invaluable team member—generous with his time, and willing to do whatever he could to benefit students. He was busy all day preparing the grounds for an upcoming weekend event. Before he left, he stopped by the principal's office and volunteered his weekend time (without compensation) to help supervise the activities. It was clear that he enjoyed his work and knew his contributions were valued.

TAKE ACTION

Ask teachers and support staff to rate the school based on the statements in the following chart.

5 = always; 4 = very often; 3 = sometimes; 2 = rarely; 1 = never	
My work title: _____	
Student learning is the common purpose of this school.	5 4 3 2 1
Everyone in the school plays a part in student learning.	5 4 3 2 1
I play an important role in supporting student learning.	5 4 3 2 1
My contributions to student learning are valued.	5 4 3 2 1
I contribute to student learning in the following ways:	
What actions are needed to create a culture focused on student learning?	

Questions for Reflection

- Do school personnel operate with a common purpose of student learning? Is this something you need to address?
- What examples of common purpose would visitors to the school share?
- What evidence of common purpose would they see in the office, the corridors, the cafeteria, the school yard, and the classrooms?
- What rituals, ceremonies, and traditions take place in the school? Which ones give evidence that student learning is the purpose of the school?
- What and who are rewarded, recognized, and celebrated? How is learning rewarded, recognized, and celebrated?
- Do support personnel feel they make a contribution to student learning? Have you asked them how they feel or how they would like to contribute?

Tip 16

Be a Leader of Teaching and Learning

Teachers and students benefit when principals function as learning leaders, rather than instructional leaders.

—DuFour, 2002, p. 13

More than ever, principals need to be leaders in improving instruction, making sure all students are learning. Schools exist to facilitate learning for students of all ability levels. The influence of the school's leader is second only to classroom instruction in its impact on student learning.

Few principals would disagree with the importance of their role in student learning. Most principals entered administration for that reason—they wanted to improve conditions that facilitated student learning. Their challenge, however, is finding time to do so. Public demands for school reform, heightened expectations, and increased accountability have changed the landscape of school leadership.

Principals find it increasingly difficult to find time to work with teachers to improve instruction. Teachers need and want assistance, but also realize the competing demands of the principal's job. A special education teacher explained, "A principal needs to be an instructional leader, not just a building manager. Unfortunately, the many tasks of the job often leave little time in this area. Discipline, parents, and meetings can quickly consume a principal's time."

In spite of competing demands, successful principals are active participants in the instructional process. They are aware of students' instructional needs and they know what kind of instruction occurs in their buildings. They find time to visit classrooms, they discuss instruction with teachers, and they talk with students about their learning. They implement the following practices in their schools:

- High expectations
- Standards-aligned curriculum
- Standards-based assessment
- Safety nets for students
- Distributed leadership
- Professional development linked with pedagogy

Principals' visibility in classrooms and hallways, consulting with teachers and talking with students, speaks volumes about student learning as their number one priority. Students in their schools know that the principal is interested in them and what they learn. A fourth grader told us, "Our old principal came to our classroom and talked with us about what we were learning. She helped us if we were having problems with math. Our new principal must not know how to do her job yet because we hardly ever see her."

WHAT THE RESEARCH SAYS

> *There are virtually no documented instances of troubled schools being turned around without intervention by a powerful leader. Many other factors may contribute to such turnarounds, but leadership is the catalyst.*
>
> —Leithwood et al., 2004, p. 4

In years past, the role of the principal, and corresponding administrative training were primarily focused on managerial aspects of operating the school. During the last twenty-five years, the role of the principal as instructional leader has emerged as a key component (Goodlad, 1979; Marzano, 2003; Sergiovanni, 1994). Today, both roles are viewed as important to school success; both are reflected in the Interstate School Leaders Licensure Consortium's (ISLLC) *Standards for School Leaders* (1996).

Research tells us that "principals' abilities are central to the task of building schools that promote powerful teaching and learning for students" (Davis et al., 2005, p. 3). Davis and colleagues suggest that closer links should be made between teacher preparation and principal preparation to provide more continuity between effective teaching and the responsibilities of principal as instructional leader. Leithwood et al. (2008) state that school leadership is a close second to teaching as an influence on student learning and has the greatest impact in schools where circumstances are most challenging and learning needs of students most serious.

According to Leithwood et al. (2004), leaders influence student achievement through their influence on other people or features in the organization, and their influence on school process by engaging in the following behaviors:

- Developing people: enabling them to do their jobs effectively by providing the training and support they need.
- Setting directions for the organization: developing and living shared goals, monitoring organizational performance, and promoting effective communication.
- Redesigning the organization: Creating a productive school culture, modifying structures, and building collaboration.

Knuth and Banks (2006), who developed the essential leadership model, assert that "successful principals do not just dash into schools as instructional leaders; rather, they work from the basics upward, taking their staff members and the rest of the school community with them" (p. 16). The overlapping nature of the ISLLC standards leaves principals who want to be instructional leaders in a quandary of what is most important and where to begin. Knuth and Banks suggest that instructional leadership is at the top of the hierarchy; before school leaders can lead successful instructional change, they must be able to articulate the school's moral purpose, have managerial support in place, and have created a sense of ownership and collective purpose among staff. These underlying elements are necessary to foster organizational readiness and capacity required to complete the final ascent to school improvement.

Leithwood et al. (2004) suggest that successful school leaders achieve impact through the following initiatives:

- Charting a clear course that everyone understands
- Establishing high expectations and tracking progress
- Developing people with support and training
- Establishing a school environment that supports and facilitates teaching and learning

According to Elmore (2003), knowing the right thing to do is the main challenge of school improvement. Schools do not fail due to lack of effort; they fail because they do not do the right work. Some schools make the mistake of changing structures assuming that instructional practice will follow (Elmore, 2002). Elmore argues that changing instructional structure does not change practice. Schools that succeed know what kind of instructional practice they need and then develop a structure to support it. They use a systematic process of accounting for what is occurring, including teacher observation and analysis of performance data. They select a target that is ambitious enough to stimulate improvement and establish external benchmarks to measure change. Finally, instructional leaders know and model instructional skills and curriculum knowledge. A model that can assist principals in identifying focus areas to improve student achievement is available in *What Works in Schools: Translating Research Into Action* (Marzano, 2003).

Although researchers and practitioners agree that school leaders need to be involved in teaching and learning, time is the biggest deterrent. The role of the principal has grown exponentially during recent years. DeVita (2005) asserted,

> [Principals] need to be educational visionaries, instructional and curriculum leaders, assessment experts, disciplinarians, community builders, public relations experts, budget analysts, facility managers, special programs administrators, and expert overseers of legal, contractual, and policy mandates and initiatives. They are expected to broker the often-conflicting interests of parents, teachers, students, district office officials, unions, and state and federal agencies, and they need to be sensitive to the widening range of student needs. (Opening letter, para. 1)

Some would argue that the number of management tasks leaves little time to attend to meaningful instructional improvement. Samuels (2008) reported that investigators who shadowed principals for a week discovered that managerial duties allowed them to spend only a third or less of their day interacting with teachers and students; the nature of the contact was too brief and unfocused to lead to instructional improvement. A national project, funded by the Wallace Commission, is aimed at improving school leader's effectiveness by placing school administration managers (SAMs) in schools to assume managerial tasks. This gives principals time to focus on becoming good instructional coaches and work with teachers to improve instruction. Launched in 2002 in the Jefferson County, Kentucky, school district, by 2008 the initiative had spread to eight states (Samuels, 2008).

WHAT WORKS IN PRACTICE

The time challenge was mentioned by all of the principals we interviewed. One principal's remarks summarized their sentiments:

Teaching and learning … [are often last on the list] in the real life of a principal and school. If you can get to the teaching and learning, which is why we went into this in the first place, it would be phenomenal. But all of these other pieces, operation, and definitely school community, get in the way and become … priorities of the day and the minute, because they seem more urgent. The teaching and learning piece sometimes gets pushed to the back.

As they shared their practices, however, many of the principals were surprised at the number of instructional activities in which they actually participated. One of them said, "This was a good opportunity for me to reflect on my efforts in this area. I didn't realize how much I was actually doing." The wide array of activities they engaged in supports the research of Leithwood et al. (2004).

Although the term "instructional leadership" has been used as a leadership model for decades, the actual practices that constitute good instructional leadership are ill defined. Principals and teachers we met agreed that involvement in teaching and learning was a key component of their role. They spoke of the importance of modeling, interacting with teachers and students to understand what was needed, and possessing curricular knowledge and instructional skills.

Principals described their practices as including

- A focus on student learning
- Modeling continuous learning
- Using data to inform practice
- Creating structures that support emergence of learning communities
- Using reading groups as catalysts for discussions
- Using off-campus retreats to bring people and ideas together
- Being in the classrooms
- Talking about learning with teachers and students

Principals shared how they led instruction in their schools:

You have to be a model for your staff. It's especially important if you have young teachers with potential, but little experience. It's hard; but if you do your job, it's worth it.

Teachers have to see you as a teacher—someone who has the skills. Not someone who was in the classroom decades ago and hasn't progressed beyond writing on a slate. They want a leader who has instructional skills, who sees their needs, and works with them to meet those needs. After we have a staff development presentation, we discuss the ideas presented, consider ideas we can implement, and discuss everybody's suggestions. You need to be viewed as a real instructional leader.

I walk through everybody's classroom every day just to keep in touch. I sit with different groups of students sometimes. It's amazing what you can pick up on. I walk through, sometimes chat with children, have a talk with the teacher. It's all very informal. If I have a chance, I give the teacher feedback; most of them I see in the mornings. If I don't have a chance to have a substantial conversation with the teacher, I stop by the classroom later. Sometimes they seek me out to discuss a related issue. "You know when you were in the room, did you see such and such ... ?" It gives them an opening to address problems with me. This is better than finding out about a problem four weeks down the track. You are more approachable because you have just been there.

[Because I spend one afternoon each week] in one of the classrooms, I am aware of teachers' accomplishments and am able to comment on them. Being in the classrooms offers opportunities to interact with students, to actually gauge their progress, and gives me firsthand knowledge from which I can discuss learning issues with teachers.

Principals reported the importance of spending time with students: "It takes a ton of work, but it is worth it!" A high school principal noted that discipline problems diminish when the principal has a positive relationship with students, treats them fairly, and does not overreact when they make mistakes. Her philosophy, "You screwed up; this is the consequence; we move forward." Elementary and middle school principals reported strategies such as taking students to lunch, treating students to ice cream sundaes on their birthdays, and having book clubs.

Teachers reminded us:

The principal must be "the teacher of teachers." He or she must want to be personally involved. I had a great principal once who always asked me to relate my educational philosophy to what I was doing; he challenged my ideas at times; he helped me become a better teacher.

A principal, new to a building, needs to learn about the instructional methods, and curriculum and assessments currently being used.

Principals need to make sure that students and instruction come first and every decision is based on the question, "Is this what is best for our students?"

My principal challenges me to think more deeply about my instructional strategies. When I have a new idea I want to implement, his questions include, "Tell me why? What are you anticipating as a result? How will you know it worked? What will you do if you don't see the results you want?" I appreciate this because it forces me to have a solid basis for instructional decisions and use data to evaluate their effectiveness. Now when I have an idea, I prepare in advance for these questions.

Principals need to communicate high expectations, raise the bar for instruction.

Coming to my class to observe, even for short periods of time, lets me know he cares about me and my class.

My principal takes an interest in what I am teaching; we have conversations that are not just about evaluations.

Teachers noted the importance of principals interacting with students:

I know their time is limited, but I think it is critical for principals to spend time interacting with students in the classroom. Students love to share what they are learning, and it sends the message that the principal thinks it is important enough to spend time learning with them.

I have had two principals who modeled good interactions with students. One of the principals knew the names of all 600 students in the building, called them by name. He had a fish tank in his office; kids he thought needed a little attention were invited to feed the fish—his excuse to visit with them and send them off on a positive note. Those fish got fed a lot of food! He also had a principal's pride board where he posted students' work and gave them a principal's pride certificate.

My principal stands outside at the bus stop every day of the year. This serves the dual purpose of crowd control and also makes him the first school person the students see every day.

At least once in the three years students spend at our middle school, they go out to lunch with the principal. He takes about 12 students at a time. I think it is a fabulous idea because he learns valuable information and keeps the data on it. He asks questions about students' perceptions about feeling welcome at school, feeling safe, being bullied, treatment by school personnel, and relevance of the curriculum. Students feel so special when it is their time to go to lunch and share their experiences with him.

TAKE ACTION

In God we trust; all others bring data.

—Ellers and Camacho, 2007, p. 629

Use the following chart to identify which of these activities you can use to improve instruction in your school.

Activity	*What Format Will I Use?*	*When Can I Schedule Time?*
Sharing what I learn with faculty		
Encouraging teachers to conduct action research in classrooms		
Creating a learning community		
Creating faculty reading groups		
An off-campus retreat		
Spending time in classrooms		
Talking with teachers about learning		
Talking with students about what they are learning		
Other activities?		

Use the next chart to detail the instructional improvements that are needed.

Instructional Improvement	Supporting Data	Action Steps	People Involved	Target Date	Assessment

Questions for Reflection

- How would your teachers rate you as an instructional leader?
- How much time did you spend interacting with teachers and students last week? How much time would you like to spend?
- How can you adjust your schedule to allow more time for instructional improvements?
- What instructional improvements are needed in the school?
- What kind of data do you collect to assist in determining needed improvements?
- How will you determine the "right work" to do?

Tip 17

Link Professional Development With Teaching and Learning

Those who strive to turn good into great find the process no more painful or exhausting than those who settle for just letting things wallow along in mind-numbing mediocrity.

—Collins, 2001, p. 208

The key to the survival of any organism is continual adaptation to changing circumstances. Teachers and school leaders are no different in this regard. Teachers, school staff, and school leaders who plan to succeed tomorrow need to be learning and updating today. Failure to grow is not only a disservice to students, but a peril for one's continued growth and subsequent employment.

Whether we embrace change or not, it happens and life continues to move forward. The only choice is to embrace change, adapt to new circumstances, or be left behind in a cloud of dust. The key is learning to cope, to adjust; in other words, continue learning. If anyone on your staff, including you, has not engaged in some form of professional growth for the last year or two, it is time to get moving. Although one's first thought is the leader and the teachers, do not forget about the staff, such as office, custodial, and cafeteria personnel. Running a school is a team effort, and everyone will benefit from learning about new products, techniques, strategies, and ideas for improving their work and personal lives.

WHAT THE RESEARCH SAYS

According to Senge (1990), organizations learn through individuals who learn (p. 130). New personal meaning and individual choice are central to school improvement. Fullan (1993) tells us that the personal meaning teachers attach to improvement is central to effective change. Davis, Darling-Hammond, LaPointe, and Meyerson (2005) note that successful school leaders influence student achievement through development of effective teachers and implementation of effective organizational processes.

Professional development for principals is equally important. Leadership training for principals needs to begin with quality mentoring and continue with professional development that meets the needs of evolving schools and districts (Wallace Foundation, 2008).

WHAT WORKS IN PRACTICE

Principals shared their ideas about linking teachers' and principals' professional development with student learning:

Look at anecdotal and hard data from a lot of sources; brainstorm; look at needs, and decide where development needs to occur. Consider your overall mission and goals as part of the decision process.

When I meet with teachers, I discuss their goals and how they align with school and system goals. The conversation is about what they have been working on this week to meet their goals. I ask if there is anything I can do to support them.

Teachers should be assisting each other with ideas, mentoring each other, sharing their expertise. They have opportunities to share during our professional development sessions. We have an experienced staff with a wealth of expertise that we use to the fullest benefit.

We found when we brought in presenters that different teachers were at different stages. So we divide into groups and have teachers attend different sessions [geared to their readiness level]. We also invite teachers with expertise to share. It encourages people to come forward and share.

In the early days, everyone did all of the professional development together. Now we identify a number of people who want to attend a particular session and send them. The number of people requesting to attend sessions has increased because they can select topics that interest them. When teachers return from professional development sessions, they share what they learned with the group.

Sometimes you can stimulate professional growth by creating a need to know or have. When I introduced projectors into the classrooms, I did so a few at a time and provided instruction on how to use them. As some teachers began to use them, others saw the advantages, and wanted them.

I am having an inservice session with several facilitators knowledgeable in technology. Teachers will be able to select sessions according to their stage of development—people who know a lot, people at the beginning. That will be a day when people can seek out the sessions they need depending on their stage of learning.

People are a very big investment. You need to keep them satisfied and working productively. Putting your time and money into ensuring that's happening makes economic sense. Train them; give them the skills they need.

The most important staff development day we have is the one we do on spirituality. We go away so it becomes a bonding experience also. Everybody goes because I make it attractive enough and I say this is important. ... We go away and we have a day where there is a speaker and time for reflection. Teachers can't give what they haven't got, and it's very important to us.

We have changed staff meetings to address only curriculum issues. Other information is handled with quick morning briefings.

We have professional development meetings twice a week. Sometimes it's the whole group; other times we divide into small groups for grade-level meetings. The focus is on quality teaching related to learning—our specific goals, assessment of where we are, and what needs to happen to reach them.

I have changed faculty meetings to more focused staff development meetings. Instead of informational meetings, I am trying to raise the expectation of what we talk about—making our meetings more about learning, where we want to go, what we need to do, and what they articulate as needs. That gives me a way to focus on what we are actually doing and examining our practices. For instance, there is a custom in the school of dressing up once a week. I asked the teachers to tell me how having a fancy dress day once a week is directly linked to student learning. We are about learning; what does this have to do with our vision and goals? We need to focus on doing things because they are in alignment with what we have set out to do—our vision.

TAKE ACTION

Professional Development Plan for Staff

Use the following chart to design a professional development plan for the staff.

Professional Development Activity	Data Supporting Need	Link to Student Learning	Target Audience	Activities

Professional Development Plan to Improve My Leadership

This chart is for you to design your own professional development plan.

Professional Development Activity	Target Date	Data Supporting Need	Activity	Link to Student Learning

Questions for Reflection

- What kinds of professional development did you use this year?
- Who was involved in the professional development?
- What data supported the need?
- What data supported improvements in student learning?
- Describe your professional development activities to improve your leadership.

Tip 18

Invest Time in Developing Teacher Leaders

Principals no longer have the time or expertise to do-all and be-all. In an ever-changing world, the talents of many are needed to prepare students for success.

Although principals may welcome teacher leaders, the bureaucratic structure of schools often does not lend itself to the emergence of teacher leaders. Providing time for development activities and collaboration is a challenge that requires creativity. Principals may need to acquire skills in establishing an environment that supports and facilitates the emergence of teacher leadership. These skills may include listening, questioning, guiding, collecting and analyzing data, and collaborative decision making. Principals may need to enhance their role as leaders and supervisors of teachers.

If the primary purpose of schools is student learning, the primary task for the principal should be working collaboratively with teachers to facilitate and improve instruction. The structure of schools and the many demands on the principals' time may make that process difficult; however, successful principals view student learning as their primary objective. They find creative ways to facilitate collaboration among teachers and spend time engaged in student learning.

WHAT THE RESEARCH SAYS

A 2008 Wallace Foundation report suggests that the new paradigm for school leaders has changed from "soloist to conductor" (p. 1). Schools that "get the job done" are not led by the virtuoso soloist, but rather leaders capable of developing the talents of others and coordinating the efforts of many in pursuit of a common goal. They are the conductors who lead schools to excellence.

Schools serve a society that is continually changing. To prepare students to live and work in this society, teachers must continue to expand their abilities and assume ever-greater leadership responsibilities. Principals must become the conductors of a supportive environment that encourages teacher development, collaboration, and celebrates the contributions of teacher leaders (Ash & Persall, 2000).

Sachs (2007) contends that while teacher leadership has emerged as a topic of interest, it is not a new phenomenon. Teachers demonstrate a variety of forms of leadership on a daily basis. Teacher leadership has become an umbrella term meaning different things to different authors. York-Barr and Duke's (2004) definition is perhaps the most comprehensive: "Teacher leadership is the process by which teachers, individually and collectively influence their colleagues, principals and other members of school communities to improve teaching and learning practices with the aim of increased student learning and achievement" (pp. 287–288).

Sachs (2007) suggested the emergence of teacher leaders requires the existence of the following cultural conditions:

- Shared norms and values
- Collaborative practices among staff and leaders
- Mutual respect and trust between stakeholders
- Open lines of communication
- A belief in continuous learning
- Time and opportunities to share
- Opportunities to celebrate achievements

The most important activities of teacher leaders are improving and enhancing teaching and contributing to the overall development of their peers. Teacher leaders have the potential to transform the nature of the teaching profession. However, it is important to clarify role responsibilities and expectations for teacher leaders and administrators to avoid turf wars and ensure that the activities of both improve the quality of teaching and learning outcomes of students.

Formative leadership theory, developed by Ash and Persall (2000), indicates that the new model of teacher leadership embraces the notion that teaching itself is a fundamental leadership activity and rejects the traditional notion that leadership is performed only by department heads, mentors, and curriculum directors. In this new paradigm, the principal's role is to foster a climate in which teacher leadership will flourish. The formative leader must possess facilitation skills and be able to imagine future possibilities, examine shared beliefs, use data, and engage faculty in conversations about teaching and learning. Everything that happens in the school should be designed to facilitate teachers' ability to design and deliver quality learning experiences. The main function of the principal is to engage in conversations with teachers, in and out of the classroom, about teaching and learning. Direct supervision of teachers' work, although needed, is less important than working collaboratively with teachers in planning and guiding instruction. Ash and Persall (2000) further note that positive school change is interactive and occurs when the following practices are in evidence:

- A clear framework for teaching and learning
- Shared governance and problem solving
- Standards-based practices
- In-school opportunities for collaboration
- Use of data to drive decision making
- Action research used by teachers to examine their work (p. 19)

WHAT WORKS IN PRACTICE

Principals described the importance of recognizing talent, investing time, and offering opportunities—large ones and small ones—to develop teacher leaders. Their sentiments are summarized in the following statement:

> It comes down to recognition and opportunity, recognizing the talents in people. Sometimes teachers don't seek leadership until somebody puts their trust and faith in them. I have had teachers tell me, "I didn't have faith in myself, but you did, and it sparked my confidence." One of the greatest joys is having staff members bring forth ideas for innovative school improvement.

Teachers reported the importance of these opportunities. One teacher said, "The opportunities my principal has given me, such as heading committees and cadres, and being interim principal in his absence have enabled me to extend my leadership skills."

Strategies principals used to develop teacher leadership abilities included the following:

- Placing teachers with leadership ability in key positions within the school, including dean positions, department chairs, grade-level leaders, mentors, student teacher supervisors, lead teachers, and committee chairs
- Encouraging teachers with leadership potential to take additional course work
- Mentoring future leaders
- Sending teachers to conferences with expectations that they will share information when they return
- Creating learning communities in which teachers assume ownership of their own learning and development
- Initiating a peer review process as part of the professional development program

TAKE ACTION

New Teacher Leader Initiative

Create a plan to foster the development of teacher leaders for the school.

Leadership Activity	Date Initiated	Purpose	Teacher	Training	Assessment

Questions for Reflection

- What does teacher leadership mean to you?
- How do teachers define teacher leadership?
- What are the benefits of teacher leadership?
- What are the obstacles to teacher leadership?
- What leadership opportunities are provided for teachers who are "ready" to assume more leadership in the school?
- How can these teachers' leadership abilities be used in the school?

Tip 19

Reflect On and Celebrate Your Accomplishments

The principalship is strewn with obstacles, fraught with challenges, but priceless in its rewards. Those who venture into the career require the patience of Job, the tenacity of Atlas, the compassion of Mother Teresa, and most important—a sense of humor.

One principal reminded us, principals have to have the

Four Ps: positivity, patience, prudence, and prayer. Positivity—because teachers and parents want to be around someone who makes them feel good about their work and school. Patience is needed to deal with so many people with so many different personalities and needs. Prudence—because it is the job of the principal to make the best decisions for the school; not the easier or most popular, but decisions that make the school more effective and learning more possible. Prudence—to keep the school legally [and fiscally] sound. Prayer—because you will meet many people you cannot help in any way other than offering a prayer.

He added:

Principals need to learn not to take things personally. You cannot win everyone over. You are dealing with highly personal and emotional topics: children and education. And you are asking students and parents to do things they might find uncomfortable: Do their work, pay attention, be respectful, or face consequences. You can be the most logical person with the most clear answer, and it won't matter [or be clear] to some.

The nature of the principalship is such that there will always be problems to solve, always something else that needs doing, and a bottomless stack of papers on your desk.

Accomplishments are easily obscured and overlooked when days are fraught with student issues, upset parents, frustrated teachers, and the roof is leaking. Principals can become disheartened when all they see is the next looming problem and fail to realize the good they have done, the success that has occurred, and that, in spite of complainers, the silent majority is pleased.

Many of the principals we met used reflection to ward off discouragement and generate the encouragement needed to move forward. One of them wrote a detailed annual school report at the end of every year. She kept a copy of the annual reports in a folder and periodically reviewed them when she felt she was "making no progress." One high school principal kept a journal; another high school principal maintained her curriculum vitae in which she detailed the positive changes she brought to the school. An elementary principal said she kept positive letters and notes from students, parents, and teachers and read them when she felt disheartened. A middle school principal added, "My secretary is wonderful about prompting me to reflect. When I seem discouraged, she quickly reminds me of the problems that existed when I came to the school and all of the improvements I have made during my tenure."

All of the principals we talked with spoke passionately about their dedication to their schools, their students, and their profession. One of them summarized, "I love being a principal. ... It can be very stressful, but it is also very fulfilling. The important thing to remember is [that] every day you are making a positive difference in the lives of students." The principalship is indeed priceless in its rewards.

Appendix

A COLLECTION OF VALUES TO GET YOU STARTED

- Identify values that are meaningful to you
- Add values not listed
- Define what your values mean

Acceptance	Accessibility	Accomplishment
Accountability	Accuracy	Achievement
Acknowledgment	Adaptability	Advancement
Adventure	Affection	Altruism
Ambition	Approachability	Approval
Attractiveness	Balance	Beauty
Belonging	Calmness	Candor
Capability	Challenge	Change
Charity	Cheerfulness	Collaboration
Command	Commitment	Communication
Community	Compassion	Competence
Competition	Composure	Concern for Others
Confidence	Confidentiality	Consideration
Consistency	Contentment	Control
Conviction	Cooperation	Courage
Courtesy	Creativity	Credibility
Decisiveness	Democracy	Dependability
Determination	Devotion	Dignity
Directness	Discernment	Discipline

Discretion	Dynamism	Ecological Awareness
Education	Effectiveness	Efficiency
Elegance	Empathy	Empowerment
Energy	Enthusiasm	Equality
Ethical Practice	Excellence	Excitement
Experience	Expertise	Fairness
Faith	Fame	Family
Flexibility	Forgiveness	Fortitude
Frankness	Freedom	Friendships
Fun	Gallantry	Generosity
Gentleness	Giving	Grace
Gregariousness	Happiness	Harmony
Health	Helpfulness	Holiness
Honesty	Honor	Independence
Initiative	Inner Peace	Innovation
Integrity	Intellectual Status	Intuition
Involvement	Justice	Kindness
Knowledge	Leadership	Learning
Liberty	Life	Love
Loyalty	Making a Difference	Money
Motivation	Openness	Optimism
Orderliness	Organization	Originality
Patience	Patriotism	Peace
Perfection	Perseverance	Persuasiveness
Physical Challenge	Piety	Poise
Politeness	Positive Attitude	Power
Practicality	Predictability	Presence
Prestige	Problem Solving	Professional Growth
Professionalism	Progress	Public Service
Punctuality	Purity	Purpose

Recognition	Reflection	Relationships
Reliability	Religion	Reputation
Resourcefulness	Respect	Responsibility
Results Oriented	Reverence	Rigor
Risk-Taking	Sacrifice	Safety
Security	Self-control	Self-discipline
Self-reliance	Self-respect	Serenity
Service	Simplicity	Sincerity
Skillfulness	Social Justice	Solitude
Spirituality	Spontaneity	Stability
Status	Strength	Success
Teamwork	Thoroughness	Timeliness
Trust	Truth	Understanding
Unity	Variety	Virtue
Vision	Vitality	Wealth
Wisdom	Work	

TRAITS AND STRATEGIES OF SUCCESSFUL PRINCIPALS: FROM THE PERSPECTIVE OF TEACHERS

Proactive	Visionary	Visible in building
Visits classrooms	Knows teachers personally	Gets to know students
Trustworthy	Builds relationships	Builds on teachers' strengths
Empowers teachers	Supportive of teachers	Positive force in school climate
Supports convictions with actions	Outwardly calm	Honest
Good sense of humor	Confidential	Talks with teachers
Assists rather than criticizes	True to values and philosophy	Good listener

Decisive—owns the decision	Fair	Consistent in behavior
Remembers what it is like to be a teacher	Foresees consequences of actions, the details as well as the vision	Optimistic
Unites people—able to create teams	Instructional leader	

TRAITS AND STRATEGIES OF UNSUCCESSFUL PRINCIPALS: FROM THE PERSPECTIVE OF TEACHERS

Disconnected from staff and students	Micromanaging	Negative demeanor
Playing favorites	Actions dictated by ego	Seldom leaving office
Few personal interactions with staff	Showing favoritism	Not giving straight answers
Reclusiveness	Lack of backbone	Not dealing with staff negativity
Inability to think outside the box		

References

Albano, C. (2008). Self mastery. Retrieved on June 6, 2008, from http://www.leader-values.com/content/detail.asp?ContentDetailID=238

Allen, T. D., Herst, D. E. L., Bruck, C. S., & Sutton, M. (2000). Consequences associated with work-to-family conflict: A review and agenda for future research. *Journal of Occupational Health Pyschology, 5*(2), 278–308.

Armour, M. (2007). *What is trust-centered leadership?* Retrieved September 7, 2009, from http://www.trustispower.com/tcl/tcl-description.htm

Aronson, E., Wilson, T., & Akert, R. (1999). Self-justification and the need to maintain self-esteem. In E. Aronson, T. Wilson, & R. Akert (Eds.), *Social psychology* (pp. 191–199). New York: Longman.

Ash, R. C., & Persall, M. (2000). The principal as chief learning officer: Developing teacher leaders. *NASSP Bulletin, 84*(616), 15–22.

Bacal, R. (2010a). *Team building: When teams aren't important or desirable.* Retrieved February 6, 2010, from http://work911.com/articles/teamdesi.htm

Bacal, R. (2010b). *Understanding the cycle of change, and how people react to it.* Retrieved February 7, 2010, from http://work911.com/articles/changecycle.htm

Barth, R. S. (2006). Improving relationships within the school house. *Educational Leadership, 63*(6), 9–13.

Bass, B. M. (1985). *Leadership and performance beyond expectations.* New York: Free Press.

Bass, B. M., & Avolio, B. J. (1994). *Improving organizational effectiveness through transformational leadership.* Thousand Oaks, CA: Sage.

Beatty, B. R. (2006, November 27–30). *Leaning into our fears: A new masters course prepares principals to engage with the emotions of leadership.* Paper presented at the annual conference of the Association for Active Educational Researchers (AARE), Adelaide, Australia. Retrieved October 5, 2009, from http://www.aare.edu.au/06pap/bea06516.pdf

Belmonte, A., & Cranston, N. (2009). The religious dimension of lay leadership in Catholic schools: Preserving Catholic culture in an era of change. *Catholic Education: A Journal of Inquiry and Practice, 12*(3). Retrieved from http://escholarship.bc.edu/ojs/index.php/catholic/article/view/851.

Blanchard, K., Carew, D., & Parisi-Carew, E. (1991). *The one minute manager builds high performance teams.* New York: William Morrow.

Blanchard, K., & Hersey, P. (1996). *Organizational behavior: Utilizing human resources.* Englewood Cliffs, NJ: Prentice Hall.

Blanchard, K., Zigarmi, P., & Zizarmi, D. (1985). *Leadership and the one minute manager.* New York: William Morrow.

Blasé, J., & Blasé, J. (1999, August). Principals' instructional leadership and teacher development: Teachers' perspectives. *Educational Administration Quarterly, 35*(3), 349–378.

Boesch, K. (2009, October). Lessons in everyday leadership. *Journal of Women in Educational Leadership, 7*(4), 169–174.

Bolman, L. G., & Deal, T. E. (1991). *Reframing organizations: Artistry, choice, & leadership.* San Francisco: Jossey-Bass.

Branson, C. M. (2007). The effects of structured self-reflection on the development of authentic leadership practices among Queensland primary school principals. *Educational Management Administration and Leadership Journal, 35*(2), 227–246.

Brock, B. L., & Fraser, J. (2001). Principals and pastors: Sharing school leadership: Perspectives from Nebraska and New South Wales. *Catholic Education: A Journal of Inquiry and Practice, 5*(1), 85–100.

Brock, B. L., & Grady, M. L. (2002). *Rekindling the flame: Principals combating teacher burnout.* Thousand Oaks, CA: Corwin.

Brock, B. L., & Grady, M. L. (2007). *From first-year to first-rate: Principals guiding beginning teachers* (3rd ed.). Thousand Oaks, CA: Corwin.

Brock, B. L., & Grady, M. L. (2009). *From difficult teachers to dynamic teams.* Thousand Oaks, CA: Corwin.

Bryk, A. S., & Driscoll, M. E. (1985). *An empirical investigation of the school as community.* Chicago: University of Chicago, Department of Education.

Bryk, A. S., & Schneider, B. (2002). *Trust in schools: A core resource for improvement.* New York: Russell Sage.

Burmeister, M. (2008). *From boomers to bloggers: Success strategies across generations.* Fairfax, VA: Synergy.

Burns, J. (1978). *Leadership.* New York: Harper & Row.

Chaplin, W. F., Phillips, J. B., Brown, J. D., Clanton, N. R., & Stein, J. L. (2000, July). Handshaking, gender, personality, and first impressions. *Journal of Personality and Social Psychology, 79*(1), 110–117.

Coffin, W. S. (1973, June 25). The nation: The Coffin course in ethics. *Time Magazine.* Retrieved August 18, 2008, from http://www.time.com/time/magazine/article/0,9171,907443,00.html

Collins, J. (2001). *From good to great: Why some companies make the leap and others don't.* New York: HarperCollins.

Cook, T. (2001). *Architects of Catholic culture.* Washington, DC: National Catholic Education Association.

Curtis, M. J., & Stollar, S. (2002). Best practices in system-level change. In A. Thomas & J. Grimes (Eds.), *Best practices in school psychology IV* (pp. 223–234). Washington, DC: National Association of School Psychologists.

Davis, S., Darling-Hammond, L., LaPointe, M., & Meyerson, D. (2005). *School leadership study: Developing successful principals.* Stanford, CA: Stanford University, Stanford Educational Leadership Institute. Retrieved May 17, 2010, from http://www.srnleads.org/data/pdfs/sls/sls_rr.pdf

Deming, W. E. (1986). *Out of crisis.* Cambridge: MIT Center for Advanced Engineering.

DeVita, C. (2005). *Getting the facts on school leadership preparation.* In S. Davis, L. Darling-Hammond, M. LaPointe, & D. Meyerson (Eds.), *School leadership study: Developing successful principals* (Opening letter, para. 1). Stanford, CA: Stanford University, Stanford Educational Leadership Institute. Retrieved May 17, 2010, from http://www.srnleads.org/data/pdfs/sls/sls_rr.pdf

Dubin, R. (1956). Industrial workers' worlds: The "central life interests" of industrial workers. *Journal of Social Issues, 3,* 131–142.

Duffee, L., & Aikenhead, G. (1992). Curriculum change, student evaluation, and teacher practical knowledge. *Science Education, 76,* 493–506.

DuFour, R. (2002, May). Beyond instructional leadership: The learning-centered principal. *Association for Supervision and Curriculum Development, 59*(8), 12–15.

Ellers, A. M., & Camacho, A. (2007). School culture change in the making: Leadership factors that matter. *Urban Education, 42,* 616–637. Retrieved October 3, 2010, from http://uex.sagepub.com

Elmore, R. F. (2002, January/February). The limits of "change": Supporting real instructional improvement requires more than fiddling with organizational structures. *Harvard Education Letter, 18*(1). Retrieved June 6, 2010, from http://www.hepg.org/hel/article/195

Elmore, R. F. (2003). *Knowing the right thing to do: School improvement and performance-based accountability.* Washington, DC: NGA Center for Best Practices.

Eltis, K. J., & Crump, S. J. (2003, December 1). *Time to teach, time to learn: Report on the evaluation of outcomes assessment and reporting in NSW government schools.* Sydney: New South Wales Department of Education and Training.

Eudaimonism. (n.d.). In *New world encyclopedia.* Retrieved from http://www.newworldencyclopedia.org/entry/Eudaimonism

Farber, B. (1991). *Crisis in education.* San Francisco: Jossey-Bass.

Festinger, L. (1957). *A theory of cognitive dissonance.* Stanford, CA: Stanford University Press.

Freedman, S. G. (2007, July 4). So much paperwork, so little time to teach. *New York Times.* Retrieved March 10, 2010, from http://www.nytimes.com/2007/07/04/education/04Education.html?_r=1

Fullan, M. G. (1992, February). Visions that blind. *Educational Leadership, 49*(5), 19–22. (ERIC Document Reproduction Service No. EJ439278)

Fullan, M. G. (1993a). *Change forces: Probing the depths of educational reform.* Bristol, PA: Falmer.

Fullan, M. G. (1993b). Why teachers must become change agents. *Educational Leadership, 50*(6). Retrieved March 30, 2010, from http://www.csus.edu/indiv/j/jelinekd/EDTE%20227/Fullen%20change.pdf

Fullan, M. G. (1997). The complexity of the change process. In M. G. Fullan (Ed.), *The challenge of school change* (pp. 33–56). Arlington Heights, IL: Skylight Professional Development.

Glickman, C. D., Gordon, S. P., & Ross-Gordon, J. M. (2010). *SuperVision and instructional leadership: A developmental approach* (8th ed.). Boston: Allyn & Bacon.

Goleman, D. (1995). *Emotional intelligence.* New York: Bantam.

Goodlad, J. I. (1979). *What schools are for.* Bloomington, IN: Phi Delta Kappa Educational Foundation.

Greenleaf, R. K. (1970). *The servant as leader.* Indianapolis, IN: Robert Greenleaf Center.

Greenleaf, R. K. (1977). *Servant leadership: A journey into the nature of legitimate power and greatness.* New York: Paulist.

Greenleaf, R. K. (1991). *The servant as leader* (Rev. ed.). Indianapolis, IN: Robert Greenleaf Center.

Gronn, P., & Rawlings-Sanaei, F. (2003). Principal recruitment in a climate of leadership disengagement. *Australian Journal of Education, 47*(2), 172–184.

Gurr, D., Drysdale, L., & Mulford, B. (2006). Models of successful principal leadership. *School Leadership and Management, 26*(4), 371–395.

Hall, G. E., & Hord, S. M. (1987). *Change in schools: Facilitating the process.* Albany: SUNY Press.

Hallinger, P., & Heck, R. H. (1996). Reassessing the principal's role in school effectiveness: A review of the empirical research. *Educational Administration Quarterly, 32*(1), 27–31.

Hallinger, P., & Heck, R. H. (2002). What do you call people with visions? The role of vision, mission and goals in school leadership and improvement. In K. Leithwood & P. Hallinger (Eds.), *Second international handbook of educational leadership and administration* (pp. 9–40). Dordrecht, Netherlands: Kluwer Academic.

Hargreaves, A. (1994). *Changing teachers, changing times: Teachers' work and culture in the postmodern age.* Toronto: Ontario Institute for Studies in Education Press.

Heenan, J. (2003, September 30–October 2). *Lessons from the past, models for the future.* Preconference address at the Second National Character Education Conference. Retrieved June 05, 2009, from http://www.cornerstonevalues.org/2003pre.html

Henson, K. T. (2010). *Supervision: A collaborative approach to instructional improvement.* Long Grove, IL: Waveland.

Herley, W. (2009). Motivating the generations: Economic and educational influences. *Journal of Inquiry & Action in Education, 3*(1), 1–21.

Hersey, P., Blanchard, K., & Johnson, D. E., (2001). *Management of organizational behavior: Leading human resources.* Englewood Cliffs, NJ: Prentice Hall.

Hoy, W. K., & Miskel, C. G. (2008). *Educational administration: Theory, research, and practice* (8th ed.). New York: McGraw-Hill.

Huberman, M. (2005). Teacher burnout in black and white. *New Educator, 1,* 153–175.

Hutchings, P. (2009, October). *Network marketing tip #5: Don't be a loser (loner).* Retrieved January 18, 2010, from http://www.articlesbase.com/marketing-tips-articles/network-marketing-tip-5-dont-be-a-loser-loner-1398699.html

Ingersoll, R. M. (2003). *Is there a teacher shortage?* Seattle, WA: Center for the Study of Teaching and Policy. Retrieved from http://www.ctpweb.org

Interstate School Leaders Licensure Consortium. (1996). *Standards for school leaders.* Washington DC: Council of Chief State School Officers.

Irons, E. J., & Aller, W. (2007). Relationship building: Navigating the future through practice: Implications for administrator preparation. In L. K. Lemasters & R. Papa (Eds.), *At the tipping point: Navigating the course for the preparation of educational administrators: The 2007 yearbook of the National Council of Professors of Educational Administration* (pp. 217–223). Lancaster, PA: DEStech.

Knuth, R. K., & Banks, P. A. (2006). The essential leadership model. *NASSP Bulletin, 90*(4), 4–18. (DOI: 10.1177/0192636505283855)

Kossek, E., & Ozeki, C. (1998). Work-family conflict, policies, and the job-life satisfaction relationship: A review and directions for organizational behavior-human resources research. *Journal of Applied Psychology, 83*(2), 139–149.

Kotter, J. P. (2009, April). Leading change: Why transformation efforts fail. *Harvard Business Review*. Retrieved Feb. 1, 2010, from http://dme.medicine.dal.ca/dme-features/docs/0910/April12-JournalClubArticleA.pdf

Kouzes, J. M., & Posner, H. Z. (2002). *Leadership challenge* (3rd ed.). San Francisco: Jossey-Bass.

Kurtzman, J. (2010). *Common purpose: How great leaders get organizations to achieve the extraordinary.* San Francisco: Jossey-Bass.

Lambert, L. (1998). *Building leadership capacity in schools.* Alexandria, VA: Association for Supervision and Curriculum Development.

Lampton, B. (2002). How to make a strong first impression: Seven tips that really work! *Expert Magazine.* Retrieved August 31, 2008, from http://www.expert-magazine.com/artman/publish/article_22.shtml

Leithwood, K. (1994). Leadership for school restructuring. *Educational Administration Quarterly, 30*(4), 498–518.

Leithwood, K., Harris, A., & Hopkins, D. (2008). Seven strong claims about successful school leadership. *School Leadership and Management, 28*(1), 27–42.

Leithwood, K., Louis, K. S., Anderson, S., & Wahlstrom, K. (2004). *How leadership influences student learning* [Executive summary]. New York: Wallace Foundation. Retrieved May 18, 2010, from http://www.wallacefoundation.org/sitecollectiondocuments/wf/knowledge%20center/attachments/pdf/howleader-shipinfluences.pdf

Luft, J. (1970). *Group processes: An introduction to group dynamics.* New York: National Press Books.

Marzano, R. J. (2003). *What works in schools: Translating research into action.* Alexandria, VA: Association for Supervision and Curriculum Development.

McLaughlin, M. J., & Warren, S. H. (1992). *Issues and options in restricting schools and special education programs.* Reston, VA: Council for Exceptional Children. (ERIC Document Reproduction Service No. ED350774)

Miles, M. B., & Huberman, A. M. (1994). *Qualitative data analysis: An expanded sourcebook* (2nd ed.). Thousands Oaks, CA: Sage.

Minnesota Department of Employment and Economic Services. (2008). *Dress and grooming for job success.* Retrieved August 25, 2008, from http://www.deed.state.mn.us/cjs/dress.htm (this forwards automatically to http://www.positivelyminnesota.com)

Moore, T. O. (2009). *Teacher perceptions of the benefits of teacher collaboration and an analysis of indicators of potential teacher attrition.* Unpublished master's thesis, Brigham Young University, Provo, Utah.

Morrison, E. E. (1966). *Men, machines, and modern times.* Cambridge: MIT Press.

Mulligan, J. T. (1999). *Catholic education: The future is now.* Toronto, ON: Novalis.

Newmann, R., & Wehlage, G. H. (1995). *Successful school restructuring: A report to the public and educators.* Washington, DC: American Federation of Teachers.

Nickse, R. S. (1973). *How to change the schools from inside: Teachers as change agents.* (ERIC Document Reproduction Service No. ED084224)

No Child Left Behind Act. (2001). Retrieved March 10, 2010, from http://www2.ed.gov/policy/elsec/leg/esea02/index.html

North Carolina Association of Educators. (2001). *Time to teach: Position paper.* Retrieved March 10, 2010, from http://www.ncae.org/cms/Time+to+Teach/122.html

North Central Regional Educational Laboratory. (1995). *Critical issue: Leading and managing change and improvement.* Retrieved from http://www.ncrel.org/sdrs/areas/issues/educatrsleadrship/le500.htm

O'Connor, E. C. (2004). Leadership and emotions: An exploratory study into the emotional dimension of the role of the post-primary principal in Ireland. *Educate: The Journal of Doctoral Research in Education, 4*(1). Retrieved October 6, 2009, from http://www.educatejournal.org/index.php?journal=educate&page=article&op=viewFile&path%5B%5D=79&path%5B%5D=76

O'Donovan, E. (2009, September). Managing generational diversity. *District Administration: Solutions for School District Management.* Retrieved from http://www.districtadministration.com/viewarticle.aspx?articleid=2122

Pascale, R. T., & Sternin, J. (2005). Your company's secret change agents. *Harvard Business Review, 73*(55), 72–81.

Rath, T. (2007). *Strengths finder 2.0.* New York: Gallup.

Riggio, R. E., & Reichard, R. J. (2008). The emotional and social intelligences of effective leadership. *Journal of Managerial Psychology, 23*(2), 169–185.

Rosenholtz, S. J. (1989). *Teachers' workplace: The social organization of schools.* New York: Longman.

Sachs, J. (2007, September 9). *Teachers for the 21st century: Leading and learning for improvement.* Keynote address presented at Teaching Australia conference, Gold Coast, QL.

Salovey, P., & Mayer, J. D. (1990). Emotional intelligence. *Imagination, Cognition, and Personality, 9,*185–211.

Samuels, C. A. (2008, February). Managers help principals balance time. *Education Week: Focus on Leadership & Management.* Retrieved May 27, 2010, from http://www.edweek.org/login.html?source=http://www.edweek.org/ew/articles/2008/02/13/23sam_ep.h27.html&destination=http://www.edweek.org/ew/articles/2008/02/13/23sam_ep.h27.html&levelId=2100

Schein, E. H. (1985). *Organizational culture and leadership.* San Francisco: Jossey-Bass.

Senge, P. (1990). *The fifth discipline.* New York: Doubleday.

Senge, P., Kleiner, A., Roberts, C. R., Ross, R. B., & Smith, B. J. (1994). *The fifth discipline fieldbook: Strategies and tools for building a learning organization.* New York: Doubleday.

Sergiovanni, T. J. (1994). *Building community in schools.* San Francisco: Jossey-Bass.

Sergiovanni, T. J. (2009). *The principalship: Making reflective decisions* (6th ed.). Boston: Allyn & Bacon.

Shulman, L. S. (2004). Autonomy and obligation: The remote control of teaching. In L. S. Shulman (Ed.), *The wisdom of practice: Essays on teaching, learning, and learning to teach.* San Francisco: Jossey-Bass. (Original work published 1983)

Siegel, R. (1998). *Fabulous first impressions: Unlatching the four-second window.* Retrieved August 25, 2008, from http://buildyourleaders.com/articles/firstimpressions.php

Sisyphus. (2010). *Encyclopedia of Greek mythology.* Retrieved February 24, 2010, from http://www.mythweb.com/encyc/entries/sisyphus.html

Smith, P A., & Nuzzi, R. (2007). Beyond religious congregations: Responding to new challenges in Catholic education. In G. R. Grace & J. M. O'Keefe (Eds.), *International handbook of Catholic education: Challenges for school systems in the 21st century* (Vol. 1, pp. 103–124). Dordrecht, Netherlands: Springer.

Smith, W., & Andrews, R. (1989). *Instructional leadership: How principals make a difference.* Alexandria, VA: Association for Supervision and Curriculum Development.

Spillane, J., Halverson, R., & Diamond, J. (2004). Towards a theory of school leadership practice: Implications of a distributed perspective. *Journal of Curriculum Studies, 36*(1), 3–34.

Stellar, K. A. (1988). *Effective schools research: Practice and promise.* Bloomington, IN: Phi Delta Kappa.

Streich, M. (2009, February 1). *Effective school leadership promotes success.* Retrieved January 8, 2009, from http://www.suite101.com/content/effective-school-leadership-promotes-success-a93561

Strizek, G. A., Pittsonberger, J. L., Riordan, K. E., Lyter, D. M., & Orlofsky, G. F. (2006). *Characteristics of schools, districts, teachers, principals, and school libraries in the United States: 2003–2004. Schools and staffing survey* (Report No. NCES 2006-313 Revised). Washington, DC: U.S. Government Printing Office. (ERIC Document Reproduction Service No. ED495419)

Tobin, K., & McRobbie, C. J. (1996). Cultural myths as constraints to the enacted science curriculum. *Science Education, 80,* 223–241.

Topchik, G. S. (2001). *Managing workplace negativity.* New York: AMACOM.

Vail, P. V. (1996). *Learning as a way of being: Strategies for survival in a world of permanent white water.* San Francisco: Jossey-Bass.

Vandenberghe, R., & Huberman, M. (1999). *Understanding and preventing teacher burnout: A sourcebook of international research and practice.* New York: Cambridge University Press.

Van Driel, J. H., Beijaard, D., & Verloop, N. (2000). Professional development and reform in science education: The role of teachers' practical knowledge. *Journal of Research in Science Teaching, 38*(2), 137–158.

Villani, S. (2008). *Are you sure you're the principal?* (2nd ed.). Thousand Oaks, CA: Corwin.

Wallace Foundation. (2008, June). *Becoming a leader: Preparing school principals for today's schools.* New York: Author.

Watzlawick, P., Beavin Bavelas, J., & Jackson, D. D. (1967). Pragmatics of human communication: A study of interactional patterns, pathologies, and paradoxes. New York: W. W. Norton.

York-Barr, J., & Duke, K. (2004). What do we know about teacher leadership? Findings from two decades of scholarship. *Review of Educational Research, 74*(3), 255–316.

Young, P. (2006, September/October). Been there, done that—and won't do it again. *Principal, 86*(1), 18–21.

Zemke, R., Raines, C., & Filipczak, B. (2000). *Generations at work: Managing the clash of veterans, boomers, xers, and your workplace.* New York: AMACOM.

Additional Resources

BOOKS

Augenstein, J. J. (2008). *Leaders in times of trial and eras of expansion*. Washington, DC: National Catholic Educational Association.

Augenstein, J. J., Kauffman, C. J., & Wister, R. J. (Eds.). (2003). *One hundred years of Catholic education: Historical essays in honor of the centennial of the National Catholic Educational Association*. Washington, DC: National Catholic Educational Association.

Bolman, L. G., & Deal, T. E. (2002). *Reframing school leadership: A guide for principals and teachers*. Thousand Oaks, CA: Corwin.

Brock, B. L., & Grady, M. L. (1995). *Principals in transition: Tips for surviving succession*. Thousand Oaks, CA: Corwin.

Brock, B. L., & Grady, M. L. (2002). *Avoiding burnout: A principal's guide to keeping the fire alive*. Thousand Oaks, CA: Corwin.

Brock, B. L., & Grady, M. L. (2004). *Launching your first principalship*. Thousand Oaks, CA: Corwin.

Brock, B. L., & Grady, M. L. (2006). *Developing a teacher induction plan*. Thousand Oaks, CA: Corwin.

Grace, G. R., & O'Keefe, J. M. (Eds.). (2007). *International handbook of Catholic education: Challenges for school systems in the 21st century*. Dordrecht, Netherlands: Springer.

Groome, T. (1996). What makes a school Catholic? In T. McLaughlin, J. O'Keefe, & B. O'Keefe (Eds.), *The contemporary Catholic school: Context, identity and diversity* (pp. 107–125). Washington, DC: Falmer.

Hunt, T. C. (2000). History of Catholic schools in the United States: An overview. In T. C. Hunt, T. E. Oldenski, & T. J. Wallace (Eds.), *Catholic school leadership: An invitation to lead* (pp. 34–58). New York: Falmer.

Hunt, T. C., Oldenski, T. E., & Wallace, T. J. (Eds.). (2000). *Catholic school leadership: An invitation to lead*. New York: Falmer.

United States Conference of Catholic Bishops. (2005). *Renewing our commitment to Catholic elementary and secondary schools in the third millennium*. Washington, DC: Author.

WEBSITES

American Association of School Administrators (AASA). A professional organization for school system leaders: superintendents, principals, and those supporting public school leadership.
http://www.aasa.org/

Association for Supervision and Curriculum Development (ASCD). A nonprofit, nonpartisan membership association that provides expert and innovative solutions in professional development, capacity building, and educational leadership essential to the way educators learn, teach, and lead.
http://www.ascd.org/

Catholic School Leadership Program, Creighton University. An online program serving principals who need additional preparation in the mission of Catholic schools.
http://www.creighton.edu/ccas/education/programs/endorsements/leadership/index.php

Marzano Research Laboratory (MRL). A resource to help educators promote student learning.
http://www.marzanoresearch.com/

Mid-continent Research for Education and Learning (McRel). McRel is a nonprofit agency dedicated to improving education through applied research, products, and services.
http://www.mcrel.org/

National Association of Elementary School Principals (NAESP). A resource for elementary and middle-level principals.
http://www.naesp.org

National Association of Secondary School Principals (NASSP). A resource for secondary principals.
http://www.principals.org/

National Catholic Education Association (NCEA). A professional organization providing leadership and service to help fulfill the mission of the church.
http://www.ncea.org

Wallace Foundation. Exists to "support and share effective ideas and practices to improve learning and enrichment opportunities for children."
http://www.wallacefoundation.org

Index

Pages followed by f indicate a figure.

NOTES

NOTES

NOTES